VISUAL

skiing

**Doug DeCoursey
and Darwyn Linder, Ph.D.**

DOUBLEDAY
New York London Toronto Sydney Auckland

V I S U A L
skiing

ESSENTIAL MENTAL
AND PHYSICAL
SKILLS FOR THE
MODERN SKIER

PUBLISHED BY DOUBLEDAY
a division of Bantam Doubleday Dell Publishing Group, Inc.
666 Fifth Avenue, New York, New York 10103

DOUBLEDAY and the portrayal of an anchor with a dolphin are trademarks
of Doubleday, a division of Bantam Doubleday Dell Publishing Group, Inc.

Library of Congress Cataloging-in-Publication Data

DeCoursey, Doug.
  Visual skiing : essential mental and physical skills for the modern skier /
by Doug DeCoursey and Darwyn Linder.—1st ed.
      p.   cm.
  1. Skis and skiing—Training. 2. Skis and skiing—Psychological
aspects. 3. Visualization. I. Linder, Darwyn E. II. Title.
GV854.85.D37   1990
796.93—dc20   90-34285
                              CIP
  ISBN 0-385-41276-2

Book Design by Stan Drate/Folio Graphics

November 1990

First Edition

CUR

The authors would like to dedicate this book to the memory of Ernest H. (Ernie) Blake, founder and spirit of Taos Ski Valley. Some people build their lives and dreams only in order to find personal happiness. Ernie built his dream so that others could find happiness through learning and sharing the mountain experience.

ACKNOWLEDGMENTS

We would like to thank Taos Ski Valley and the Ernie Blake Ski School for their patience and support. We also thank Jean Mayer, technical director, for his inspiration and willingness to constantly expand the ski teaching envelope.

We are forever indebted to Ken Gallard, whose contribution goes far beyond his fabulous photography. To Gail Atchinson, our thanks for the wonderful drawings. To Ilse Mayer, our thanks for providing a place to work and enthusiastic support. To Pat Brockwell, Dave Knittle, Scott Goeller, and Debbie Kanter, our thanks for sharing your love of ski teaching with us. To Clifford C. Ross, Doug Pheiffer, Bill Lash, the staff at the National Ski Hall of Fame in Ishpeming, Michigan, Paul Adamian, Dana Brienza, Danny Brienza, Bob Gleason, and all the interested students we have been lucky enough to work with, thank you for your insights.

For the years of support and faith that ultimately led to this project, we thank Stanley and Shirley DeCoursey and Ferne and Els Linder. For aid above and beyond the call of duty, our thanks to Doug and Amy Wilsterman.

Special thanks to Robin and Patricia Klaus, Ron and Jean Pacchiana, David and Judy Stepner, Jim and Mary Burns and Bill and Carolyn Rainer for their faith and support.

We are also indebted to our editors at Doubleday, Kara Leverte, Joel Fishman, Barry Zweig and John Duff, whose assistance kept us going, and to Ray Cabe and Angela Miller of International Management Group for this opportunity.

Finally, there is a huge price paid by lovers and spouses in an undertaking such as this, so to Marie Linder and Lisa Cenotto go our deepest gratitude. Without their love and support, this book never could have been written.

FOREWORD

Much of what goes into good skiing is all tied together. Good skiing depends not only on technical aspects and the movement of your skis, but equally on the mental side and the skier's confidence. This book really brings all that together, which was exciting and refreshing for me to see and read. When I get on the hill to instruct people, I start with the basics, which include the whole mental side as well as physical and technical competence. If you don't have that, then you're not going to do technically what you want to be able to do. For an athlete at the World Cup level of skiing, it *is* a mental game. We always fine-tune on the technical side, of course, but pretty much the whole game is mental. I'm convinced that keeping this in mind can help the general public, as this book will.

For example, the indoor work in Chapter V really gets you into the right frame of mind for skiing. When you start to get the mental imagery going, you are also getting into the mode of skiing, the whole mind-frame, as well as starting to tone the muscles and getting them ready for the slopes. Another thing about doing indoor work is that if you're prepared, and if you go through the progression and take care of these steps, the stress of performing lessens. I was rarely nervous or stressed-out about my skiing, only feeling that way when I was not prepared. Performing pretty much became a luxury. After training so hard and practicing so hard, the process of performing was a relief because I could just let loose and do it. It wasn't stressful, *because* I had prepared. I think that applies to most skiers, whether you are competing or are out free-skiing.

I also really appreciate the emphasis on efficient, modern ski technique in this book. I came into skiing at a time when racing technique had already evolved to emphasize lateral movement and using the ski as a tool. But I learned about the efficiency of modern technique from a drill that we used to do on the U. S. Ski Team. We would ski nonstop runs doing slalom turns, as many tight turns as we could squeeze in between the top and the bottom of the run. After about seven runs in a row, when we were completely exhausted, we couldn't waste energy any longer and had to use good technique to continue to make quick turns. We learned what I think is really important about technique: that you don't need all that extra motion to turn the skis.

Not long ago, I was out skiing with a friend who is not a very good skier. She was pretty scared, so she began sitting back and consequently had to work really hard to do anything with her skis. I worked with her to get her into a more balanced stance, but I didn't do much more with her technique. When she was able to balance, she could use the skis more efficiently and her confidence picked up. By the end of the day we were skiing runs that she thought she wouldn't be able to ski until the end of the season, if then. I thought back to that experience when I read this book, and I can see a lot of similarities in the way the authors and I think about this sort of thing. Confidence, balance, techique—everything ties together, and I like the way this book does it.

I'm often asked to think back to the day I won the gold medal in the giant slalom in 1984 at Sarajevo, and to describe what I was feeling and thinking at that time. I had put in the time on skis over miles of practice runs, and I knew that I was physically prepared. But I was definitely peaking somehow inside, too. Looking back, it was almost a perfect example of what Doug and Darwyn say in *Visual Skiing*. In order to win that day, all aspects of my skiing had to come together—the mental and the physical. Skiers at all different levels require the same combination of technique and mental skills. The recreational skiers that I know ski to have fun, and that means skiing the terrain you want, at the speed you want, with the people you like. It's no fun to get in over your head, so you have to know your limits and build from there, gaining confidence as you gain mental and physical skills. Take your ski lesson, or use this book, and if you then go out and make one good turn, remember the feeling, and then make twenty, or fifty, turns in your mind that night. The next day you can make maybe five good turns; you keep on building from there. Good skiing is efficient, dynamic, graceful—and a lot of fun. This book combines the basics of modern ski technique with the mental skills you need to make changes in your skiing, and then to ski at your best more of the time. It will be a valuable addition to any skier's bookshelf. And you'll have more fun out on the slopes, which is what it's really all about.

—Debbie Armstrong

CONTENTS

Introduction

Perfect technique! Uncompromising style! Somewhere deep within the recesses of every skier's mind is a vision of the skier they aspire to be. For many, it is the image of an athletic Austrian ski instructor, circa 1965. We will call him Hans.

Picture in your mind's eye the graceful descent of this consummate artist. The stoic upper body is riveted straight down the mountain while at the same time moving up and down with piston-like precision. The feet are locked inexorably together, snaking rhythmically from turn to turn. The head is lifted defiantly. His total concentration is evident as his steely blue eyes sweep over the slope below. The hands provide a staccato counterpoint through the precise pole plants. The strong, resilient torso coils and uncoils as the heels are thrust laterally to and fro. Meanwhile, the skis subtly etch featherlike fans of fancy on the crystalline field of wonder. Wow! Sounds great, doesn't it? We can see it now, and you probably can too. In fact, if we were to gather a group of today's recreational skiers and show them a video of Hans' skiing, there would undoubtedly be a great number of knowing smiles and nods of appreciation. For many, this is perfect technique.

This was Austrian technique, and along with the different yet equally elegant French version it represented the state of the art in ski technique well into the 1960s. You, too, might be able to learn to ski this way. However, the commitment would be astronomical. It would require thousands of days of skiing, preferably starting as a child. You would need to find thirty-year-old equipment (modern gear does not lend itself to this style of skiing) and a coach to instruct you in its use. It would require some innate athleticism, as well as physical training, since each run would require large expenditures of energy.

The reason instructors like Hans skied so well is that they probably were on skis by the time they were three. Additionally, those that spread out across the globe to found or become involved with ski schools were often their country's very finest skiers, not to mention being in top shape. They made it look easy. However, it was anything but easy. Their sense of style truly helped build the ski industry as we know it by attracting millions to the sport, but it is important to realize that it was not their style that made them great skiers. It was their ability and experience. They would have been magnificent using any style or technique.

If this style of skiing is so difficult for ordinary mortals to master, is there another option? Yes. Run the calendar forward to one of the preeminent ski racers of the 1980s—Debbie Armstrong, for example. Picture a free skiing run by this superb athlete. The relaxed upper body is quietly balanced as she flows ever forward down the mountain. The turning impulse moves laterally from foot to foot within a comfortable, stable stance. Each pole lightly flicks the snow for an instant as the skis alternately carve precise arcs on the same crystalline field of wonder.

Despite the obvious prowess of this magnificent skier, it is entirely possible that she might go comparatively unnoticed on a crowded slope. Meanwhile Hans' style and movements might actually create a greater impact on most of the crowd. Why is it that one of the greatest skiers of the 1980s could be overshadowed by a twenty-five-year-old flashback? Because modern skiing is subtle. It most often requires only minuscule muscle contractions and subtle adjustments of balance. More than ever before, the modern super-skier makes it look easy—possibly too easy to see the nuances. It just is not as visually arresting.

On the other hand, you could see and appreciate what Hans was doing. His combination of power and grace was wonderfully seductive. This contrast takes nothing away from either skier. They both represent leading-edge technique, given their respective time frames.

It is certainly reasonable to believe that a skier such as Armstrong has been exposed to a great number of techniques, styles, and coaches throughout her skiing career. Why, then, does she choose to ski in this manner? For that matter, why do racers from virtually every country ski in a way that results in the modern look we described? The fundamental reason is equipment. Nowhere else in skiing is the need for form to follow function so great as it is in the world of international racing. When fractions of a second mean the difference between success and failure, efficiency of movement and precision of line are paramount. This efficiency and precision has become possible since the late 1960s because of incredible refinements in skiing equipment. Later we will go into greater depth concerning equipment. Suffice it to say that modern ski technique with the equipment used by Hans would be as unproductive as his method used with today's gear.

WHY ME?

World Cup racers' choosing a particular technique or style is one thing, but why should we do so? First, because it is much easier on the body. It is more efficient, and by efficiency we mean getting the most out of the equipment with the least work from the body. This is of ultimate importance to the racer, and should be equally important to any skier. Modern technique allows us to use the natural forces present in skiing to our advantage rather than fighting against them. Modern skiing also provides greater control. A fundamental tenet of modern skiing is that the skis should most often slice arcs in the snow, not skid sideways. This benefits skiers at all levels of ability, especially in adverse conditions such as ice, crud, steep terrain, choppy bumps, and so forth. It is analogous to driving a car through a series of turns under varying conditions. Although you may skid sideways a bit on an icy or gravelly curve, it would be more desirable for the car to track precisely through the turn with the rear tires following the same path as the front tires. There are certainly times in skiing when it will be beneficial to skid. However, on those occasions skidding should be an option rather than the skier's only choice.

Another reason to adopt modern technique is that it will allow you to continue to grow as a skier. A common complaint registered by skiers at many levels is that they reach a "plateau" in their ability: "I've been skiing like this for years. Help!" The average skier skis only about ten days a year. During this time the skier typically rediscovers the same inefficient behaviors of the previous year. Continued growth in a skier's ability requires a solid foundation upon which to build. From there, it is possible to explore additional facets of skiing, such as Nastar racing, moguls, quick turns, or skiing the steeps. The mark of good skiing is versatility. Hans overcame his plateaus and became versatile through vast experience. In this book, we will help you expedite this learning process by providing you with fundamental movement patterns of modern skiing. From these sound fundamentals you will be able to develop the versatility needed to ski, as the French say, "toute neige, toute montagnes" (all snow, all mountains).

Finally, modern skiing provides the opportunity for a great deal of self-expression. Classic technique often required strict adherence to achieving a particular "look" or position at each level of development. Today, despite the fact that the best contemporary skiers use similar mechanics, they each retain a distinct and individual sense of style. The basics of modern technique do not require that you look just like your instructor. Therefore, rather than becoming a clone, use the mental and physical fundamentals presented in this volume to grow as an individual.

THE GAP

If modern technique is so much easier and more effective, why do so many skiers still seek the "classic" image of skiing? This gap exists for a variety of reasons. First, as we mentioned, classic techniques were far more visual. Learning a physical skill effectively normally involves a great deal of mimicking and visual imprinting. The old instructor's standby, "Follow me and watch what I do," helped imprint an image the skier could easily copy. However, as skiing has become more subtle and less easily demonstrated, the need for additional teaching styles and modes of learning has increased. It is now much more important that students be cognizant of particular sensations and movements in their muscles and joints. This is referred to as *kinesthetic awareness*. It is necessary since many movements in modern skiing are so small they can be felt but barely seen. It is also important that the skier understand the dynamics of modern equipment. In many ways, modern equipment looks like the equipment of old. The tips still turn up in front and skiers still wear large boots. Understanding that modern skis are designed to turn efficiently and that modern boots more effectively transmit instructions from the skier to the ski is one of the first steps toward freeing yourself from the constraint of imitating Hans.

There is something quite seductive about Hans' skiing style. It is visually accessible—you can see the movements—and it is also visually appealing. Part of this appeal was created by the marketing of this technique. Millions of images of skiers energetically hopping, twisting, and heel-thrusting were drummed into the consciousness of the skiing public. And repetition leads to acceptance. However, there is also an innate attractiveness to the classic ski technique. It had *style*—like Fred Astaire and Ginger Rogers, like a tuxedo worn with elegant grace, like a 1965 Mustang convertible. Like all these things, classic ski technique still appeals to us today. In fact, it is still fun to ski that way—for a little while. But the appeal of those "featherlike fans of fancy" has kept many skiers from appreciating the wonderful efficiency of modern technique used with modern equipment. Even when given good instruction on modern gear, many skiers are unable to use it effectively. Though they don't quite realize it, they are trying to ski like Debbie Armstrong while a vision of Hans dominates their minds. This gap between a vision of classic style and the reality of modern technique is a source of frustration to skiers and instructors alike. We hope to help you attain a clear vision of modern skiing while still cherishing the memory of Hans, for he and all those he represents were great skiers.

Yet another reason for the persistence of dated movements is that modern movements are not as intuitively sensible as their older counterparts. The experience of attaching long boards to our feet has few parallels in life. When asked to change direction with these apparent impediments, certain predictable human behaviors appear. These behaviors are most closely aligned with classic technique. To see a skier make a turn by jumping up and powerfully twisting the upper body relative to the lower body does indeed make sense if you want those darn boards to turn. Since turning is an excellent way to avoid obstacles, it is important to our well-being that we have a powerful and effective way to turn. The movements of classic technique fit nicely with our intuition of how to turn with boards on our feet. The more subtle movements of modern skiing, though ultimately more effective, don't fit nearly as well with what we think we have to do. We often use the following example: Suppose you are flying down a slope and a tree suddenly appears in your path. Who are you going to trust—your instincts, which with all their frailties at least have kept you alive thus far, or an instructor who has told you that by gently applying pressure to the inside edge of the ski and patiently guiding your foot in the intended direction you will turn and, incidentally, save your neck? The point is that the use of strenuous twisting, explosive unweighting, or another seemingly obvious response does not necessarily imply that a skier is stupid or unathletic. It merely suggests that the skier is sincerely attempting to change direction or slow down. Not to worry. Modern technique requires less energy and provides far more control. Once familiar with the effectiveness of these movements, the body and mind gratefully accept them.

The final and possibly most sinister cause of "the gap" is that most skiers' friends have a seemingly uncontrollable desire to pass on their wisdom in the form of tips. Many skiers receive information based on older techniques, which has been handed down from skier to skier for years, even decades. The information is usually inappropriate and dated, and often just plain wrong. These tips usually seek to correct a problem by addressing the effect of the problem rather than the cause. For example, a common lament in moguls is that for the first few turns a skier does well, but then suddenly loses control, leans back and shoots across the slope. The friend's advice is often, "Hey, don't lean back." Yet the problem probably started with the way the first turn was made. Leaning back was only the logical consequence of a sequence of events, and thus the friend's "tip" is useless. The problem never would have occurred if the skier had learned to initiate a turn effectively. The friend's advice is like telling a drowning man not to breathe while under water. Again, the problem never would have occurred if the man had learned to swim. Possibly it would have been better to get him out of the water! No one questions the motives of these amateur "teachers." However, we definitely question the results.

The tips or hints given are usually not consciously designed to re-create the "picture of Hans." The "teacher" is often unaware of the dated nature of the tips. They often come as tidbits, such as "Always keep your feet together," or "Always face straight down the hill," or, our personal favorite, "Always lean forward as far as you possibly can." These Band-Aid type fixes seldom work, even if the information is valid. Tips are ineffective because they seldom deal with the fundamental skills necessary for efficient modern skiing. When the tip is based on dated information the problem is compounded.

How do we escape the flood of well-intentioned tips? Read and utilize this book and then take lessons from a respected ski school. Another valuable source of help is to videotape a World Cup giant slalom and then watch it in slow motion. Remember, the speed at which these skiers move produces some exaggeration. However, no matter what country the skier hails from, you will see quality, efficient movements worth copying.

THE PROCESS

How do we learn to ski? How can we learn to ski better? How do we break bad habits? How can a book help this process? Great questions. If the answers were simple, everyone would know them.

There is one indispensable component of modern skiing—balance. However, it is not a simple notion. The term "balance" is often thrown around rather loosely, and often leaves the reader with a nebulous idea of how it may be achieved. Everyone who skis has balance, so why do we need a book, instructor, or video to teach it to us? Because balance means more than merely standing up through the course of a run. In this book, balance will refer to the functional positioning and movement of the body to allow effective control of the skis. As skiers begin a run, they choose a stance that is designed to facilitate the movements they intend to bring to bear to turn their skis. The movements they use are a product of past learning (tips, classes, books, imitation) as well as their intuitive beliefs concerning appropriate movements. The effect of these movements on balance is seldom considered, and it is often disruptive. Stance and movements that maximize the body's innate ability to maintain balance must be developed. Only then is the skier able to view skiing from a functional sense rather than from a sense of style or blind adherence to others' "tips."

This book will review the history of skiing, equipment, and technique to help provide some background about how and why we ski the way we do today. We will then present a straightforward approach to maintaining a more relaxed state of mind when facing stressful skiing situations. Next we will help you develop the ability to use imagery and visualization in order to master and apply new skills. Then we will explore the movements fundamental to modern skiing. Particular attention will be paid to making the skier aware of the importance of stance in achieving the elusive goal of balance. Finally, we will help skiers apply these skills when they reach the slopes. It is our belief that for most people a lengthy, encyclopedic volume that details hundreds of possible movements a skier might want to use is relatively ineffective. We believe that the true value of this book is that it can help skiers at virtually any level by providing clear mental and physical templates of the basics of modern skiing. Just as professional sports teams spend large amounts of time honing fundamentals, we believe that basic movement patterns can have the most impact on skiers' performances. The intent of providing this information is not to turn every skier into a clone reflecting these beliefs; on the contrary, establishing quality fundamental skills will allow each skier to optimize his or her own particular style. We believe that virtually any person will make correct and high-quality choices if able to approach skiing from solid fundamentals. We have never worked with a student who did not possess the physical talent to achieve reasonable goals in skiing. People are amazing, and their bodies react beautifully if given half a chance.

Those who have difficulty in skiing up to their potential often cite overcoming their fear as a major problem. How will we deal with fear? The best way to conquer fear in skiing is to have a fundamentally sound and versatile means of turning your skis. Making complete, round turns is the most effective way to control speed and maintain balance. A positive attitude is wonderful; however, confidence in one's ability to turn is the most effective way to overcome unproductive fear and anxiety. The chapters on progressive muscle relaxation and imagery skills will also be useful in developing skiing abilities. Being fearful of skiing that depends on shaky skills is not a sign of a lack of courage on the skier's part. It is a sign of intelligence.

BASIC ASSUMPTIONS

To underscore some of the basic themes of this book and to briefly acknowledge some of our other fundamental beliefs, we hold these truths to be self-evident:

- The vast majority of skiers worldwide ski recreationally. Therefore, our top priority is to help them derive the most enjoyment possible from the fabulous sport of skiing—in other words, to have more fun. It may take the form of overcoming plateaus in learning, conquering new terrain, learning to ski fast, making more precise turns, or just sharing great moments on the slope with good friends. Skiing safely, in control and with efficiency of movement, is certainly more fun than the alternative.

- Equipment innovations over the last twenty-five years have dramatically changed skiing.

- Virtually everyone has the basic physical ability to ski effectively.

- Effective skiing movements must begin from a centered and balanced, open stance, which is maintained and adjusted with movements of the feet and lower body.

- The movements of modern skiing, although physically easier and far more efficient, are not immediately apparent either visually or intuitively.

- Modern skiing emphasizes a movement pattern in which lateral movements of the lower body are used to control the skis. The actions begin in the feet and move up through the body as needed.

- Skiers should try not to accept "tips" from friends. Simply smile and say "Thank you for sharing that with me." If technical assistance is required, take lessons from a ski school with a good reputation.

- The process of developing the fundamental movements of modern skiing can be enhanced through simple exercises at home. Imagery skills and an ability to reduce tension in the body can further expedite this process.

• Exercises designed to reorient skiers to their equipment and to the basics of modern skiing can be of great value during the first days of each season and can provide the foundation for skiing each year.

• If it isn't fun, it shouldn't be done.

The Development of Modern Ski Technique

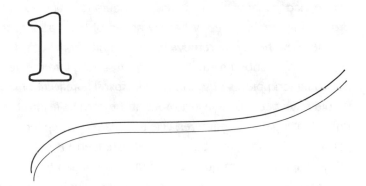

Before moving into the modern equipment and technical revolution, let's first go back in time. The setting is the cold plains of what we now call Sweden, circa 2500 B.C. The order of the day was survival. The idea of recreation was still nebulous at best. Imagine a cold, gray morning in which twenty-six inches of fresh snow has fallen overnight. Our hero, a seminomadic hunter/gatherer and father of two, is contemplating a day of trudging through knee-deep snow in search of game. This, then, begins the fable of:

ULLE, THE WORLD'S FIRST SKIER

Ulle had already been awake for hours, splitting wood, making a fire, and generally procrastinating. He knew what lay ahead of him—a long, cold, miserable day of hunting—and he knew he had to retrieve his stone knife from behind the hut, where he had left it after cutting some caribou meat. To keep from sinking into the deep drifts of new snow, he tossed out some long pieces of wood he had split. He reflected momentarily on how much easier it would have been to have just brought the darn knife into the house the night before like any right-thinking hunter/gatherer. Ulle then carefully stepped on the first board with his left foot, paused momentarily for balance, and extended his right foot toward the next piece. These planks supported him quite well, but as he began to bring his right foot forward, his new reindeer-skin boot became imbedded in the rough, splintered board. The board came along with him, and rather than pull back and disengage the gnarled plank from his boot, he used

it for his next step. Besides, he had only thrown three pieces of wood onto the snow, and his left foot was already on number two. Now if he could only imbed that boot into the last piece of wood, he could get that stupid knife with minimal effort. Having already lifted his left foot from the piece supporting it, he again balanced on his right foot, and looked at the last board. Unfortunately, it was on his right-hand side and slightly ahead. He crossed his left leg over and in front of his right and deftly drove his

foot onto the splintered board. He immediately realized he had a problem. He had indeed succeeded in attaching two boards to his boots, but with his legs crossed it seemed a hollow victory. After floundering around for a minute or two he finally fell, thereby disengaging the two pieces of wood. At that point, he returned to the old-fashioned way of knife retrieval, he walked. Without realizing it, Ulle had just learned the first lesson of skiing: Don't cross your legs with boards attached to your feet. He returned to the house with his knife to warm up.

Later, during the day's hunt, Ulle kept thinking about the morning's experiment. If he could devise another way to attach the boards to his feet, not only could he move through deep snow faster but his feet would be much warmer walking on top of the snow instead of sinking down into it. When he returned home, Ulle warmed his feet and then returned to the woodpile. The first thing he had to deal with was how to attach the boards to his feet without ruining his boots. He selected two planks of roughly the same size, about three feet long and eight inches wide. He chose the smoothest he could find and, paying particular attention to the area under the foot, he further smoothed the boards with his stone axe. Both planks were a similar shape since they were both split from the same log. They both had a slight curve on one end, and Ulle brilliantly decided they should point forward and turn up. The only thing Ulle could think to use to attach his boots to the planks were loops of reindeer gut. He found the right size loop, put it around the board and slipped the front of his boot under it, and took off around the hut. It worked fairly well and, after a few laps, he knew he was onto something. The only problem seemed to be that the gut on the bottom seemed to drag on the snow. By now, it was dark. Oh well, enough innovation for one day.

The next day Ulle had another idea. This time he used a wider band of gut and attached the band to the top of the planks using small wooden pegs. Now he was ready. Grabbing his bow and other hunting implements, Ulle put on his boards and took off. It was great! Travel was much easier and faster on top of the snow and his feet were much warmer. He was psyched. Although he covered a lot of terrain, he did not find any game that day. As he headed home he found himself at the top of an incline. Ulle sensed that this situation could cause some problems, but ''what the heck'' he boldly strode forward. The snow had settled during the day and it now allowed the planks to slide easily. They shot out from under him. Ulle's immediate reaction was to lean back and attempt to dig in his heels. This did nothing to slow him down. However, he did succeed in losing his balance. Soon thereafter Ulle experienced skiing's first major crash. Ulle had learned another important lesson in skiing: Leaning back to dig in one's heels does not slow one down. This was somewhat distressing for him, but the exhilaration of movement was captivating.

The next morning Ulle collected his equipment and went out to hunt once more. This morning was much different. The wind had blown hard all night and the snow was packed. Ulle wondered how this would affect his planks. He slipped them on and took off. Soon he reached the top of a small rise. He recalled the disaster of the day before. Intuitively, he decided to angle his descent. He walked forward and the boards begin to slide. The slope was not very steep and with the added help of crossing at an angle his speed was quite comfortable. Mysteriously, though, the boards turned as he slid forward, so that by the time he was halfway down he was pointed straight down the slope. Still, his speed was manageable and, although he had no idea why his boards changed direction, he didn't care. He reached the bottom of the hill and had enough momentum to head up the side of the next slope. This quickly slowed him down, and now he found himself pointing straight up the next hill. As his skis began to slide backward, Ulle realized he had done it again. This time, however, he merely leaned over and fell to the side. Yet another valuable lesson for Ulle: If in doubt, bail out. Although he again found himself covered in snow, he was elated. The speed and exhilaration were tremendous. He was hooked.

Near the end of the winter, there was an unusually deep snowstorm which lasted three days. When it finally lifted, Ulle headed out on a hunting trip. The snow had completely erased his old tracks and he found the going tough. As the day wore on and he went farther the snow became even heavier. Ulle had struggled for hours and was going nowhere fast. He began to use his bow to push himself through the thick slop. It seemed to help, but the thin bow often sank far into the snow. Ulle realized that it would be futile to continue since even if he did make a kill he could never get it home. He turned around and headed toward the hut. Even following his old tracks was a lot of work. As he trudged on, he noticed a long,

dead branch partly torn from a tree. Maybe this would work better than the bow, he thought. Ulle grabbed the branch and ripped it from the tree. The end that came from the tree was curved and fairly wide. Ulle found this worked well. He was able to make much better time by pushing with the branch as he went. The branch became another indispensable part of Ulle's equipment arsenal. The ski pole was born.

The following autumn Ulle felt an anxious, almost giddy feeling about the approaching winter. As he prepared his wood pile for the winter he spent almost as much time selecting prime boards as he did chopping. He found a number of uprooted saplings which would be perfect for pushing. He would be ready this winter. His children were getting older and his son would soon be accompanying him on hunts, so he built boards for them. He modified his old skis to fit his wife's boots and of course selected two choice planks for his own new equipment. Let it snow, he thought. Ulle had become a skier.

Ulle quickly built up a stockpile of food and turned his attention to teaching his family how to use the boards. One morning he assembled them all outside their hut with their boards on their feet. Without a word Ulle began marching off down one of the tracks, expecting them all to follow. When he finally turned around, he saw both the children floundering in the snow and his wife had not yet moved. He turned around and came back to help the kids get up. He gave them a rather curt lecture on all they had done wrong. By now, the children were crying. His wife also appeared to be less than pleased. Ulle began to lecture once more. The family's response was immediate and unanimous. They kicked off their boards and

marched into the hut. Ulle had just learned possibly his most important lesson in skiing. Never attempt to teach immediate family members. Over the course of the winter, the children became quite proficient, although they never did use the pushing sticks Ulle had made for them. His wife even used her boards from time to time and did great. Ulle figured they all did so well from watching him, but he was wrong. Although they all had to go through a period of adjustment, trial and error had worked for them just as well, maybe even better than it had for Ulle. So much for the first ski lesson, but what can you expect from a hunter/gatherer?

This winter Ulle had a great deal more opportunity to glide downhill. There was a fairly large hill not far from the hut. Ulle would occasionally try a run after hunting or on a day off. Ulle was fascinated by the feeling he got from gliding downhill. He found that his balance was aided greatly by leaning slightly on his pole as he descended. When controlling his speed became a problem, he would lean on it a little more. During these times he also noticed that crouching down seemed to help his balance. Although he was never very graceful, he always felt a certain sense of accomplishment after negotiating a run without a fall!

During these downhill jaunts, Ulle found it necessary to change direction from time to time. Although the slope had few trees, there were ditches and boulders to contend with, particularly in the early winter. The only method of turning Ulle knew was to step his boards in the direction he wanted to go. He often employed this movement while gliding along his hunting tracks. When he encountered an obstacle he learned that stepping out of the track and stepping his planks around was a reasonable way to change direction. Unfortunately, this move was nearly impossible when going a bit faster. As he vividly remembered, leaning back didn't work, and certainly falling down to stop got very old very quickly. Ulle made some other attempts at turning. He would occasionally try twisting his upper body in the direction he wanted to go. It seemed reasonable enough; however, it almost always led to a crash. He had learned even earlier that leaning in the direction he wished to go had no effect on altering the course of the planks. He even tried twisting his upper body in the direction opposite the way he intended to go. Sometimes this was marginally effective, but these occasions were so few and far between that he soon abandoned this method as well. Once, while traveling fairly fast, Ulle found himself on a collision course with a small stand of trees. Instinctively he jumped up and quickly twisted his skis in a new direction. Although it kept him from hitting the trees, it also led to the worst crash he had ever experienced. Ulle's solution to this dilemma was to carefully point his boards in a direction with no obstacles. Effective methods for turning boards would have to await discovery for thousands of years.

Countless generations of Ulle's family kept his legacy alive. Although using the boards continued primarily as a mode of transportation and as an aid to hunting, no one who put on the boards failed to feel the sensations that had made it so exciting for Ulle. For many hundreds of years the fable of Ulle would be told when "people of the planks" would gather. They would raise their earthen mugs of hot fermented elderberry juice and toast Ulle, "the father of the plank." It is difficult to precisely trace the family tree of Ulle. But it is said that on a cold night in 1957 a descendant of Ulle's was born not far from where Ulle had first used his planks. He would grow up to be perhaps the greatest skier the world would ever know. They called him Ingemar Stenmark.

THE END

The Moral

Human beings are not born with the ability to ski. It is not immediately natural.

Trial and error allowed Ulle to eventually move around on the boards rather effectively. It is obvious that humans then and now are quite adaptable. However, Ulle's first, innate reactions tended to provide little in terms of successful results. Ulle's initial attempts at gliding downhill found him trying to dig in his heels to slow down. This is perfectly reasonable given his previous knowledge about walking down a hill. The sensation of sliding caused him to crouch down to lower his center of gravity and make him more stable. Another sensible reaction. However, both of these "natural" reactions put Ulle in a very inefficient position to change the direction of his descent. The same scenario can be observed today on any beginner hill anywhere in the world. His use of stepping to change direction while slowly gliding along the tracks was brilliant. Unfortunately, the fact that it was ineffective at higher speeds made this type of turning less than totally satisfying.

Twisting and leaning with the upper body were also natural responses in attempting to redirect the skis. However, given Ulle's equipment, these movements did not produce satisfying results. Variations of these basic movements actually became the cornerstone of techniques used throughout the world in the 1940s, 1950s, and 1960s. Refinements of these movements came to define skiing technique. They made sense and were visually clear. They helped define the golden age of skiing. Ulle was no dummy, he was just ahead of his time.

The progression of skiing from Ulle's time to the mid-1960s was logical. The allure of movements used in the early sixties is undeniable, and they were sensible. There is little similarity, however, between many of the "natural" moves of the past and the subtle manipulation of today's "planks." With the advent of plastic boots and fiberglass skis, the rules have changed. Skiers of today are asked to make movements that take advantage of the design of the tools (equipment) they have selected.

The bottom line is that those of us fortunate enough to be involved in skiing can benefit and grow from the lessons of the past, but need not endlessly repeat Ulle's experiences. Ulle would have been happy to see what he started. Let us continue to build on what he began.

HIGHLIGHTS FROM SKIING HISTORY

Skiing has a rich and fascinating history. We have used the fable of Ulle to introduce some of the themes that will be developed later in the book. In the next section we have selected (and embellished) some highlights from the last hundred and thirty years of skiing. If you are interested in more information about the development of skiing, we recommend the section on skiing history compiled by Bill Lash and Phil Britton that appears in Horst Abraham's *Skiing Right.* For those interested in the earlier history of skiing we recommend *A History of Skiing,* by Sir Arnold Lunn.

1861   The first "tech-weenie" of the modern era, Sondre Auversen Norheim, designs shorter skis (only eight feet long) and puts a "waist" in his skis, making them narrower under the foot and wider at the shovel and tail. It is not clear if these changes were intended to make the skis easier to turn or to give them better flotation in deep snow. In any case, Miller Softs and Head Standards should probably have been called "Norheims." Norheim also anchored the skier's heel to the ski with a strap of twisted willow twigs.

1866   Norheim shows he is more than just a tech-weenie; he becomes the first hotdogger by inventing the parallel stop christie. "Looking good" on skis becomes a possibility. Now everybody wants to ski (or at least stop) parallel.

1879   In the first recorded time trial in America, Tommy Todd is clocked at 88 miles per hour on Lost Sierra Mountain, in California, north of Lake Tahoe. Everybody wants to know what wax he used, but his ski tuner wouldn't talk.

1896   After experimenting with Norwegian skis, Mathias Zdarsky writes the first illustrated ski manual, *Lilienfeld Schilauf Technik.* Little does he know he has started an evolutionary process leading to this book.

1904   Victor Sohm teaches skiing in the Arlberg, using the Norwegian technique. One of his students is fourteen-year-old Hannes Schneider, who will influence the development and teaching of ski technique for the next several decades.

1909–10   Schneider invents the stem christie, in which the skis are brought into a parallel position after the turn has been initiated and the turn is completed in a parallel skid. Sohm asks, "Why do all these kids want to ski *parallel*?"

Hannes Schneider

1916–18   Schneider teaches skiing to the Austrian Mountain Troops. He makes no technical innovations, but to deal with so many students Schneider invents a brand-new kind of tyrant: the ski school director.

1923   Professor Charles Proctor sets up the first slalom course in America at Dartmouth College, unknowingly starting a collegiate ski-racing dynasty. This also gives college students everywhere ideas for winter carnivals, ski weekends, and other excuses to party down.

1928   Sir Arnold Lunn organizes the first slalom race, the Arlberg-Kandahar. He figures that if people are going to ski the same track, we may as well time them.

1930 Rudolf Lettner of Salzburg, Austria, puts metal edges on his skis to keep them from wearing out on the rocks. He finds that the metal edges also increase turning power. (Ulle would have loved these skis.)

Gustav Lantscher wins the first speed trials, called the Flying Kilometer, at St. Mortiz, Switzerland. He goes 66.4 miles per hour (everything was converted to miles per hour in those days) and immediately calls Tommy Todd to find out what wax he used.

1931 Sig Buchmayer starts the first American ski school at Peckett's Inn on Sugar Hill in Franconia, New Hampshire, teaching Hannes Schneider's Arlberg technique with its extreme down-up-down movement. He charges a dollar a lesson, setting an eternal precedent for the underpayment of ski instructors.

Sig Buchmayer

1932   Sigmund Rund, a Norwegian, schusses the headwall at Tuckerman's Ravine on twelve-foot skis, using one long pole for balance. He coins the phrase "sidecut is for sissies," but nobody understands Norwegian and the phrase is lost for two generations.

Sigmund Rund

1933   Adolf Attenhofer develops an all-metal binding that holds the heel down securely for skiing but frees it for walking. Skiers find that metal works much better than twisted willow twigs for holding the ski securely to the boot when jumping into the air to turn.

1934   Hannes Schneider teaches the Arlberg crouch, but fellow Austrian Anton Seelos coaches the French team using his technique of rotation and up unweighting. One of his racers is Émile Allais, who learns to ski with the skis almost always *parallel*. This method of skiing, jumping into the air and throwing the body around to turn the skis before landing, remains the most popular way to ski for years.

1936   Toni Ducia and Dr. Harold Reinl in Austria and G. Testa and Professor E. Mathias in Switzerland develop the concept of "twisting skiing." It is something like modern technique (steering an edged and weighted ski). Only a few skiers can demonstrate it on the equipment of the time. The French team rejects the Ducia-Reinl technique in favor of Allais's method.

1937   Émile Allais wins the FIS (Fédération Internationale du Ski) downhill and slalom with his parallel technique. It is the best way to ski on the equipment of the day, and Allais is a superb athlete. Unfortunately, his success stamps an image into the minds of most skiers and up unweighting combined with rotation becomes an *idée fixe*.

1938   The French National Ski School adopts the Allais technique. What choice do they have, *mes amis;* the man is a world champion and a national hero. In addition, Allais writes *Ski Français,* with Paul Gignoux and Georges Blanchon, spreading his ski technique worldwide.

1939–40   The Allais technique emphasizes sideslipping rather than snowplow and stem turns, and placing equal weight on both skis. The rotational forces that turn the skis are generated in the upper body but are transmitted to the skis by a blocking action of the hips. This technique worked very well with the equipment of the era. It still works today; the laws of physics haven't changed. But equipment has, and what was necessary then is superfluous now. But we're getting ahead of our story.

1942–43   The Tenth Mountain Division of the U.S. Army, headquartered at Camp Hale, trains in Colorado. There are no technical breakthroughs, but the friendships formed and the plans laid lead to the postwar boom in American skiing. The boys of the Tenth Mountain Division are a major force in the development of American skiing from the end of World War II through the present day.

1946   On December 15, the Aspen Skiing Corporation in Aspen, Colorado, opens for business with Lift One on Ajax Mountain. Ever since Norheim invented the stop christie in 1866, people have been trying to "look good." From this date forward they will have *the* place to do it.

U.S. Army Tenth Mountain Division

1947   Plastics are introduced to the ski industry in the form of the first plastic ski bases. These skis are very fast and make turning even more important.

1948   The first "Prayer to Ulla" ceremony is held at Mount Baker, Washington, on October 8. Ulla, a Scandinavian deity, is the patron saint of skiers. The prayer, to ensure deep snows and to fend off broken bones, is held around a bonfire of skis and poles that have been broken while skiing. The words of the prayer derive from ancient Norse curses that are best left untranslated. Of course, we recognize this pagan rite as deriving from Ulle's practice of burning broken planks (skis) in the fireplace of his hut.

Meanwhile, at Mohawk Mountain in Connecticut, owner Walt Schoenknecht dealt more directly with the problem of lack of snow. He had giant blocks of ice trucked in and crushed, and covered his bare slopes with the resulting slush. The next year, three intrepid souls tried mixing air and water through specially adapted nozzles, and the snowmaking industry was born.

1948–49   The first commercially successful metal ski, the aluminum Head Standard, is marketed by Howard Head. Ulle would have loved these skis; they can be thrown into a forward sideslip by merely batting an eyelash, enabling the skier to control speed without really changing direction.

Meanwhile, France and Austria continue to dominate the development of ski technique and, although there are subtle differences, both methods rely on body rotation to generate the forces that turn the skis.

1948–50   Moguls begin to appear on mountains that have never before known them. They present a new challenge to skiers, leading to the modification of skiing techniques. The extreme movements of the French technique require too much time for execution, and the skier finds himself doing face plants rather than enjoying the new challenge. The phrase, "You're late, you lose," is coined by an observant Austrian.

1948–52   The Austrians develop a technique that allows much quicker turning of the skis by what eventually becomes the counter-rotation so characteristic of the 1960s. Using the technique, the Austrians are able to ski bumps very well, and they ski slalom courses even better. Toni Spiess, Christian Pravda, Hans Nogler, and Franz Gabl, all Austrian, win international victories. The new technique begins to be picked up by other skiers, and is called, in different variants, "mambo" and "wedeln." The international flavor of skiing is firmly established when Émile Allais (French, in case you've forgotten) teaches these Austrian inventions to skiers in Squaw Valley, California, U.S.A.

1950–51   Cubco bindings become available. They are a step-in, step-out binding with excellent heel hold-down, allowing skiers to jump into the air to turn the skis almost as well as with long thongs. Unfortunately, it was possible to step out of them quite unexpectedly, leading to spectacular face plants.

1955   Buckle boots become available. The Henke Speed Fit is the precursor of today's high-tech marvels. At the time, the principal beneficiaries are boot salesmen (boot fitters hadn't been invented yet), who no longer have to endure raw, bleeding hands caused by lacing boot after boot onto a fussy customer.

Stretch pants complete the "looking good" skier's ensemble. Bogner's introduction of this style revolution means that the Lycra-encased, buckle-booted skier can click into his or her bindings and start looking good without the awkwardness of lacing up long thongs.

Stretch pants also revolutionize ski teaching. Now instructors can see what the students' knees (and other interesting body parts) are really doing. More important, students can now see more clearly how instructors turn the skis.

1956
Toni Saller wins three gold medals at the 1956 Winter Olympics at Cortina d'Ampezzo, Italy. His margins of victory are amazingly large. Everybody who is paying attention wants to ski like the Austrians, except the French, who want to ski faster than the Austrians (and will, in a few years).

Toni Sailer

1958
The Graduated Length Method (GLM) is introduced by Clif Taylor, who consulted with Harvard psychologist S. S. Stephens to develop the method, which applies basic principles of learning and perception. Soon there are thousands of short-ski fanatics on the snow, creating new kinds of weirdly shaped moguls.

Clif Taylor

1961　The French, miffed by the recent Austrian domination of international ski racing, develop "Christiania Leger." In this new technique, the upper body remains square to the skis while movements and pressures of the feet initiate and guide the turns. This may be the beginning of the modern technique, but it may also be the beginning of two divergent paths: racing technique and "national" technique. The truly efficient techniques of international ski racing will continue to develop as plastic and fiberglass revolutionize skiing equipment. But recreational skiers will be taught techniques that were necessary with soft boots and wooden skis, and that continue to be visually appealing.

1963　The Rossignol Strato 102 is one of the first of the truly high-performance, quick-turning skis that make modern technique possible. French racers begin to take advantage of these innovations and start to close the gap with the Austrians. Recreational skiers buy the skis, but try to use them with Hans's technique. Most ski schools continue to teach as though skis were designed *not* to turn.

1964　Americans Billy Kidd and Jimmy Huega win silver and bronze medals, respectively, in the slalom at the 1964 Winter Olympics. They are the first American males to win Olympic medals in alpine skiing, and the wins are a big boost for the American team.

1966　After several years of experimentation, Bob Lange is able to produce a high-performance, all plastic boot. They are bright yellow and are called "comps" in America and "les plastiques fantastiques" in Europe. Racers begin to use these and similar boots introduced by other manufacturers, which transmit subtle movements of the lower leg and foot quickly and precisely to new-generation skis. Recreational skiers use them to try to ski like Hans; so do most ski instructors.

Meanwhile, Hermann Goellner perfects his double somersault on skis. This doesn't depend on new equipment, just on Goellner's athletic ability and his healthy disregard for his own safety.

1968　Jean-Claude Killy repeats Sailer's feat, winning the gold medal in all three alpine disciplines (downhill, giant slalom, and slalom) at the Winter Olympics in Grenoble, France. He skis with a freedom of movement and relaxed upper body that is in marked contrast to the other racers. When he is closely observed, it is clear that he is simply skiing with his feet, using his boots to transmit movements and pressures to his responsive skis. Killy's skiing, and his victories, underline the effectiveness of modern ski technique. There will be detours and blind alleys, but the general direction to efficient, modern skiing has become clear.

Jean-Claude Killy

1970   The revised edition of *The Official American Ski Technique* is published. Among the seven basic principles of ski technique it lists are *forward lean* (the skier places the center of gravity *ahead* of the ball of the foot), *up unweighting*, and *counter-rotation*. These were important components of Hans' ski technique, but not of Killy's, nor of other top international racers (like Karli Schranz, who happened to be Austrian). However, some ski schools, and a few visionary instructors, begin to adapt modern technique for the use of recreational skiers.

Meanwhile, after four years of continuing disregard for his personal safety, Hermann Goellner performs a *triple* somersault on skis. Freestyle skiing is off and flying.

1971–90   The ski world is treated to a dazzling array of superb skiers from many countries. The technology of ski and boot design progresses at an almost dizzying pace. The best skiers in the world, the World Cup racers, learn to use the new equipment with an elegant efficiency, perhaps best exemplified by Ingemar Stenmark, who dominated slalom and giant slalom racing for nearly a decade. The major innovations in ski teaching, however, are pedagogical, not technical. The Americans, represented by Professional Ski Instructors of America, are leaders in this movement. Ski instruction improves due to an emphasis on developing the skills needed for skiing rather than on polishing specific maneuvers, such as short swing, to achieve a specific "look." Even so, most recreational skiers and most instructors do not adopt the technique that works so well for international racers. Ski and boot manufacturers eagerly adapt the newest technology to the

Ingemar Stenmark

needs of the skiing public, and some ski schools and instructors begin to teach the movement patterns of modern technique. Overall, however, a widening gap appears between the way the racers use boots and skis as tools for turning and the way most skiers fail to realize the full potential of the new gear. The racers are efficiently slicing arcs in the snow while the majority of skiers are energetically jumping and twisting, trying with all their might to create those featherlike fans of fancy on crystalline fields of wonder.

(Skier A)

Phil Mahre (Skier B)

THE EQUIPMENT REVOLUTION

Pictured above are two of the best skiers the world has ever seen. At the time each photograph was taken, "it didn't get any better than this." Sartorial changes aside, what are the fundamental differences between these two skiers? One of our first observations is that Skier A appears to be much lower, and is bending far more at the waist, knees, and ankles. Skier B, on the other hand, is more erect, providing for a more relaxed look. Skier A seems to be bearing down powerfully *over* the outside ski, whereas Skier B appears to be quietly balancing *against* the inside edge of the outside ski. At this point let's clarify what is meant by the inside ski versus the outside.

If we could look at how each skier initiated the turn, we would see Skier A move up powerfully to begin his turn. Skier B would have moved in a more lateral direction. The overall feel of Skier A would be one of powerful vertical movements followed by an aggressive twisting in the torso to help force the skis into each new turn. Words that describe this skiing might include hopping, twisting, pushing, unweighting, and leverage. With Skier B, we would see a relatively quiet upper body in which one ski is quietly released, whereupon the other is

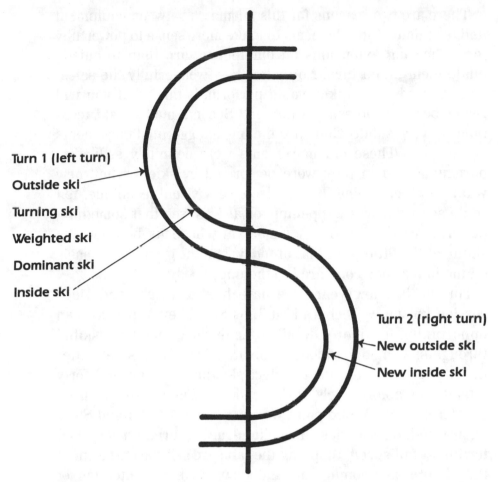

Turn 1 (left turn)

Outside ski

Turning ski

Weighted ski

Dominant ski

Inside ski

Turn 2 (right turn)

New outside ski

New inside ski

Bisecting line is used to define the end of one turn and the start of the next.

engaged. Terms describing this type of turning might include skating, flowing, gliding, and centered. Why the difference? Did we recently stumble upon the Einsteinian realm of ski technique? No, not really. Is it today's weight training or cross-training? Fitness is great, but ski racers with legs that looke like tree trunks are nothing new. Possibly the greenhouse effect has changed snow texture? Nope. Racers have always skied on ice when possible. If it is not technical insight, the individual, or the weather, what is it? Answer: equipment. Even if Skier A could have glimpsed into the future of ski technique the moves of today would have been useless on old equipment. Unfortunately, what is so often seen today is just the reverse. It is not uncommon to see skiers of today jumping, hopping, and twisting their bodies in an effort to make modern skis turn. It's a shame, since modern equipment is so effective that turning is usually less a problem than over-turning.

There are two reasons for this mismatch between equipment and technique. First, it seems to make more sense to powerfully force the long extensions on our feet to turn than to quietly guide them into a turn. No matter how wonderfully the salesman said your new skis would perform, is this what you will remember in a pressure situation? Second, modern ski technique is very subtle. Gone are the big, exaggerated movements of the past. These old movements were definitely seductive, particularly when they were performed by skiers who knew what they were doing. It was also a very visual technique. You could see what was happening, or at least see that something powerful was going on. A major shift in focus between the skiing of the fifties and that of today is in the greater emphasis on the lower body compared to the upper body.

For the last few years, we have held a lecture and video session known as Tech Talk at Taos Ski Valley. It provides an opportunity for more detailed analysis of modern skiing through slow motion video (an invaluable tool). It is held after the lifts close so as not to affect ski time, and around forty attend. The ability levels of the students range from advanced to intermediate. At one point we show a tape of Phil and Steve Mahre making a series of medium-radius turns on groomed terrain at full speed. Stopping the tape, we ask the gathering if the Mahres are coming up and down with the intention of unweighting their skis in each turn. The nods from the crowd are always in agreement with this basic premise. These guys obviously ski well, and there is obviously movement, so they must be coming up and down, right? Not necessarily. We then rewind the tape and show it again, but in slow motion. In slow motion it becomes obvious that the Mahres's upper bodies remain relatively stationary and that the activity used to turn their skis is happening primarily in their legs. The particulars of this activity will be discussed in Chapters V and VI but it is sufficient now to say that at moderate speeds on groomed terrain, skiing is predominantly a subtle, lower body activity. If this is the case, then why does a group of savvy, accomplished recreational skiers almost always perceive the Mahres's turns as having a great deal of up-and-down movement, unweighting, hopping, or whatever? One reason is that when most recreational skiers observe another skier they focus on the largest part of the picture—the upper body. Instructors and coaches, on the other hand, tend to begin their analysis of turns with how the ski interacts with the snow. As this analysis continues they move from the feet up and not from the head down. Using this scheme, it becomes much easier to see that the Mahres are mostly pressing and guiding the outside ski through one turn, releasing it, and then doing the same with the other ski. Weight is taken off the turning ski at the end of its turn, but only to make the next turn by changing weight to the other ski. As speed or the rate of turning increases, it may be necessary for the skier to tip the outside (controlling) leg inward to maintain balance. In doing this the upper body may indeed move closer to the snow, or down. Moving to the other ski (releasing) may require the torso incidentally to move up. However, these motions are a consequence of moving laterally, not of moving up and down over the ski.

This brings us to a major distinction between 1950s technique and modern skiing. Today we stand against one ski, and balance and guide the ski through the turn. In contrast, older technique required flexing deeply to prepare to extend in order to unweight the skis, so they could, essentially, be turned in the air. One sacred cow of skiing is that you must move down-up-down to turn your skis. This dovetails nicely with the ultimate ski tip: "Bend your knees." It is easy to see from this how lateral moves can be mistaken for vertical moves. Down-up-down—unweighting—is what the eye and brain are prepared to see. Do not interpret this to mean that we no longer use any flexion or extension in modern skiing. Certain applications of skiing, such as narrow chutes or thick powder, may still find us hopping energetically. It is just that we must make a distinction between lateral movements used to change weight from ski to ski and vertical movements used to lift both skis off the snow: modern versus classical, if you will. We still use flexing and extending movements, but in most cases for rather different reasons.

Finally, we return again to the fundamental reason for the change from essentially vertical movements (to make the skis light enough on the snow to turn) to lateral movements (to guide them through the turn): equipment. With tools that have turning engineered into them (modern skis) and efficient links to transmit our instructions (modern boots), all movements can be greatly minimized, and in some cases eliminated altogether, due to the sensitivity of our gear. Why are we hammering this point into the ground with fables, historical outlines, various analyses of past and present technique? Because you have to believe that what you attach to your body is more than sticks and hiking boots. You may not be able to see all these qualities, but you have to trust that they exist; otherwise all the analogies and exercises in the world will not encourage you to use your equipment as tools rather than two by fours.

The advent of plastic boots and fiberglass skis has changed the face of skiing dramatically. For the best skiers, form has certainly followed function. Traditional techniques varied much more from country to country and even from region to region. However, they all did share one major commonality. They all utilized powerful movements to make the skis turn rather than the subtle moves of today. They had to do this. Prior to the mid-1960s skis had limited turning properties. Sidecut (meaning the tip and tail of the ski are wider than the middle) and metal edges had been part of ski design for decades, but the skis were still basically boards that had to be made to obey. Leather boots were relatively ineffective in quickly transmitting pressures from the skier to the ski. Bindings were responsible only for attaching the boot to the ski, and bore little resemblance to today's safety release bindings. What modern equipment has done is provide a positive link (the boots) from the skier to their highly engineered turning tools (the skis). To make a turn, the modern skier merely needs to slide downhill, put a ski on edge, and allow the weight of the body to press against the middle of the edged ski. Because of the ski's shape, it bends in an arc and seeks to turn. Fine adjustments of the arc of the turn can then be made by applying twisting forces with the outside leg. In this case, it is the job of the skier to "ride along," balanced against the turning ski. Quite literally, the ski makes the turn and the skier merely sends the commands through the boot.

CULTURAL DIVERSITY

In the 1950s and early 1960s the two dominant ski techniques were the Austrian and the French. During this period it was relatively easy to distinguish between French and Austrian skiers. Whether it happened to be instructors, or students, reared under their tutelage, the differences were evident. The French technique displayed a very square stance with the body

French ski technique in the 1950s

Austrian ski technique in the 1950s

moving in the direction of the turn. The skis would follow the body, and the turn could be completed by flexing deeply in the ankles and knees, producing a skidded arc. As the French refined their technique in the late 1950s it became more subtle, and included *projection circulaire*, a smooth rotational movement involving the hip more extensively than in the past.

Now let's look at some of the dominant characteristics of Austrian ski technique in 1958. The following is taken from the General Preface to the Theory of Movements from *The New Official Austrian Ski System* (New York: A. S. Barnes and Company, 1958). It says concerning powerful twisting movements: "The main characteristic of the present skiing style . . . is the dominant place which the conscious outward turning of the heels occupies as the initiator of a change of direction." Concerning body positioning: "Counter-rotation and outward inclination of the upper body . . . become distinctive characteristics of the ski technique." Concerning releasing and turning: "Vorlage (or forward body position) . . . a well-timed freeing of the rear ends of the skis, so that the turning force of the heels can work properly." Concerning the position of the feet: "Proper leg action strictly demands a narrow ski track (feet close together) which, once mastered, ensures far greater security than a wide track."

Although there were early Austrian uses of rotation as well as counter-rotation, the enduring difference between systems can be viewed as rotation (French) versus counter-rotation (Austrian), and remnants of both methods can be seen in many excellent skiers today.

Although different in appearance, both systems were quite powerful in redirecting the skis. They both relied on a common principle: using the upper body to transfer powerful turning forces to the lower body in order to make the skis change direction quickly. Realize, of course, that this is a highly simplistic view of two ever-evolving ski techniques. Austrian and French skiers always have been and continue to be among the most imaginative and most copied innovators in the skiing world. Their leadership is well documented and well deserved. To some degree, there are still movement differences displayed by students of each national technique along the lines discussed above. However, these distinctions lessen with each year. It must be remembered that skiing in France, and particularly in Austria, is a major economic factor for each country.

There is a need for a unique and identifiable technique to attract and then hold customers from the continent and the entire world; in other words, for marketing. It is also the case that a career in ski teaching in these countries is just that—a career. Becoming a fully certified instructor in either country requires extensive schooling, a lengthy apprenticeship, talent, and desire. For these reasons, beliefs are strong, and distinctive characteristics of national techniques endure.

THE KICK

As we noted earlier, early versions of French and Austrian technique used powerful forces to redirect skis. We also mentioned that these kinds of turning forces seemed intuitively more sensible than those used in modern technique. Although many skiers still use undisciplined variations of the French and Austrian techniques, many modern skiers have adopted a new kind of powerful turning force. It is often seen in connection with these older beliefs about technique. We will refer to this new technical strain as "the kick." It resembles some elements of older techniques in that it utilizes a powerful force to help redirect the skis. This is essentially the lifting of the new inside ski at the beginning of the turn and rapidly pulling it toward the other ski, which causes both skis to be displaced laterally. More simply stated, it is the inside leg kicking the outside leg in order to get both skis into a turn. We often ask students why they buy expensive modern equipment if they are going to use this technique to make a turn. After all, antique skis or even two two by fours will react to this type of stimulus, so why bother spending the extra money? This comment may sound cold or callous, but it usually achieves the desired result—the undivided attention of the student to the process of learning new movements.

In all fairness, most people who use this movement don't realize they are doing it. This behavior has its roots in a classic "tip" of modern skiing. That tip is to lift the inside ski at the beginning of each turn to ensure that the weight is on the new outside ski. In and of itself, this is a wonderful concept. In fact, many superb skiers lift the inside ski to begin virtually all their turns. Super. It is a very visual concept to which budding parallel skiers can relate. The problem is that merely picking up the inside ski does very little toward initiating a turn. The goal of the skier is to turn. Lifting the inside ski does little if anything to help. The skier becomes confused, knowing that good skiers often lift the inside ski so there must be something else that makes this move helpful. It takes very little time for the skier to come up with a solution to this dilemma. When the inside ski is off the snow it is in a very effective position to kick the outside ski into the new direction. What else are you going to do with it up there in the air? There are many variations of this idea. Some intermediate skiers who predominantly lean back will move forward at the end of one turn and lift the ski momentarily so that they can displace the skis to the side before returning to their seated position. Those who lean forward excessively lift just the tail of the inside ski, pull it in, and displace the tails to begin the turn. Some skiers, particularly widetrack (wide stance) skiers, do not actually jam the inside boot against the outside boot but merely start the action and then quickly stop it, which imparts the same type of turning force (displacement) to the skis.

All right, what's so bad about this move, anyway? First, it shows that the skier does not really believe that the skis will turn unless powerfully forced to turn. Second, although this type of turning can be moderately successful on perfectly groomed intermediate slopes, it is a disaster in powder, slush, ice, bumps, race courses, or at high speed. Third, by displacing the skis to the side, the skier invariably ends up with most of their weight on the inside ski, which is exactly what they hoped to avoid by picking it up in the first place. If quizzed, almost every skier will say that it is the outside ski that controls the turn. The left leg turns right and vice versa. The kick, however, utilizes the inside ski to begin the turn and often ends up making the outside ski passive. Finally, it forces the skier to develop the habit of always keeping their new outside ski relatively flat so that the kick can have the desired result—displacement. Other than small children, beginners who have not been "taught" by well-meaning friends, and true experts (of which there are very few), virtually all skiers display this type of behavior occasionally. This tip and its inevitable consequences virtually define parallel skiing for many at the intermediate level. It is certainly the most popular "lesson" skiers teach their friends when showing them how to ski parallel. It's visual, it's hip, and their friends are still alive, so it must be right. Wrong.

Kick using forward leverage

Kick using aft leverage

The kick is even found in epidemic proportions at the instructor level. At this level it is much more refined and the practitioner, again, is usually completely unaware of its existence. At this level, the most sinister aspect of the kick is that its intensity increases geometrically as the skier senses the need to turn more quickly. Unfortunately, these occasions involve the same list of hazards we went through earlier. The results are the same for instructors as they are for anyone else: trouble.

So what do we do about it? No matter what combination of moves or techniques you use as a skier, realize that you use them due to the fact that you are a normal, thinking human being. The kick is one way the body tries to overcome the hindrances to turning with skis strapped to the feet. In a sense, that makes this movement logical. Logical, yes—effective, no. Does it work? Sort of. However, if you were blindfolded and made to ski backwards, you would get the hang of that, too,

Kick from the wide track

particularly if you only skied groomed runs. So cut yourself some slack. Do not berate yourself for less than perfect technique; realize that you merely need to overcome some basic human tendencies. This will allow you to use your modern skis as the precision turning tools they are rather than as expensive planks. It will be the addition of alternative, positive movements that will release you from the kick, not just the knowledge of its existence.

Thus skiers tend to fall into three categories: unweight-and-twisters, kickers, and modern skiers. You may have been able to identify yourself in the descriptions we have provided, or you may ski with components of all three. As we said in the Introduction, modern technique will allow you to use your equipment efficiently and elegantly and to ski with less effort and more pleasure. We hope that you are now motivated to begin the process of change.

Skiing at Your Best

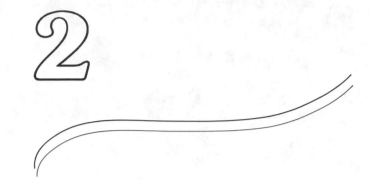

For most people skiing is recreation: fun. At least, that is what it is intended to be. Yet there is undeniable pressure to perform well. It is a highly visual and very public sport. At Taos, everybody on the number one chairlift can see who is skiing Al's Run, and everybody skiing Al's Run knows it. Performing in front of an audience is one of the classic definitions of a high-stress situation, and it is something that skiers often must do. In addition, we put pressure on ourselves to avoid falls, meet the challenges of difficult terrain, progress from beginner to intermediate to expert, handle deep powder, and on and on.

PEAK PERFORMANCE IN SKIING

So, while for most recreational skiers the quality of their performance doesn't really count, it certainly does matter. We know that it matters to our students because they tell us directly, and indirectly, by taking a lesson. We think performance probably matters to you, too. After all, you did buy this book, and you are reading it. Because performance matters, you'll enjoy yourself more if you can consistently ski at or near your best. This chapter is intended to help you do just that.

The Peak Performance Myth

Most of what sport psychologists know about peak performance comes from interviewing athletes who have done something extraordinary. When asked to remember what they were feeling or thinking or experiencing while performing, they provide accounts that have led to defining a special psychological state in which peak performances—the best we can do—most often occur. Over the last few years the term "the zone" has been used to identify this unique state, but other terms like "the cocoon" and "the flow experience" have also been used. The characteristics of this special state of mind are listed in a number of books designed to help athletes discover their peak performance state and enter it at will. After reviewing these reports, Darwyn and his fellow researchers at Arizona State University found five common themes. When you cut through the flowery or mystical language, the most often mentioned components of the peak performance experience are: (1) a clear focus of attention on the task; (2) lack of concern with the outcome; (3) effortless performance; (4) a sense of time slowing down; and (5) a feeling of confidence and invincibility. That's what it is supposed to be like to be in "the zone."

Now, all of this must be taken with a grain of salt, because the evidence for the existence of a special peak performance state consists almost entirely of the recollections of successful competitors. What if the losers on a given day said exactly the same thing as the winners? What if a given athlete said the same thing regardless of whether he or she had won or lost? What if the expectations of the interviewer prompt the athlete to respond with the standard description of the zone experience? Consider the candid response of Tommy Armour III, after he played a great round of golf on the third day of the 1990 Phoenix Open. When asked if he had been in the zone, he said that he really didn't remember anything special about his mental state because he was *so focused on playing each shot he wasn't paying attention to himself.* There is a strong possibility that many reports of the zone experience are really based on the expectations of the inteviewer, because the athlete doesn't remember his or her mental state, having been too busy attending to the task at hand. We call the process by which accounts of the zone experience have been developed "retrospective introspection," and we think that it is very unreliable. There is a good chance that the zone is a myth, and a dangerous one at that.

The Dangers of Trying to Find the Zone

We firmly believe that your state of mind has a major impact on the way you perform as a skier and in other demanding tasks. But we also believe that the search for the zone can have some negative consequences for performance. If you are led to believe that there is a special psychological state in which peak performance occurs and that when you fail to attain that state you will also fail to perform at your best, you are setting yourself up to fail with what is called a self-fulfilling prophecy. Suppose you believe in the zone, and you even convince yourself that you have found it on some occasions. "I had such an outrageous day of powder skiing; I was in the zone all day long!" Now there is eighteen inches of new powder on your favorite mountain; it's a clear, cold, beautiful day; your skis are tuned and waxed, and you get up on the slope and you can't find the zone, can't find it anywhere. What do you do? The most likely thing is that you'll have a dismal day doing body plants in that wonderful powder, because you can't find the zone and you believe that you can't ski powder unless you do find it. You'll fall because you expect yourself to fall. If you define the zone as a special, elusive, secret place, you are setting yourself up for failure. There will be a lot of times when you don't find it, and perform badly because that is what you expect will happen when you aren't in the zone. To avoid the dangers of this myth we recommend that you develop some psychological skills that help you perform at your best consistently, rather than trying to find a way to attain that mysterious state in which peak performances are supposed to occur.

PEAK PERFORMANCE SKILLS

The research that Darwyn and his colleagues have been conducting at Arizona State University has led to the conclusion that only two of the five components we listed above associated with peak performance are really important. Peak performance most often occurs when attention is clearly focused on the task and when the person is very confident of their ability to succeed. It is fortunate that these are the components you are most likely to be able to attain on a regular basis, if you develop them as skills rather than pursue them as a kind of altered state of consciousness.

Focusing Your Attention

You focus your attention all the time, but often you are not aware of doing so. If you are absorbed by what you are reading, you have been effectively focusing your attention on this book. If there is music playing in the background you probably have not been paying attention to it. But if you now choose to do so, you can hear it, and it will interfere with your paying attention to this book. Attention is limited in the sense that we can't pay attention to everything that is happening. Just as attending to the music causes you to lose your focus on this book, attending to the distractions that surround you in skiing will cause you to lose your focus on your own actions. It is true that we can do some things without seeming to pay attention, like driving a car. But tasks that have not yet become automatic, and tasks of greater difficulty or complexity, like skiing a steep bump run, require our undivided attention.

The distractions of the past, the anxieties of the future. Two of the most common ways skiers lose a clear focus of attention on skiing the terrain in front of them are to dwell on the past and to worry about the future. It is essential that you make good judgments about the terrain you intend to ski so that you don't attempt to ski runs that demand skills you haven't yet developed. However, if you are on terrain that is difficult but possible for you, a review of past failures, or a lurid preview of the consequences of a fall, will divert your attention from accomplishing what you intend to do: to ski the run to the best of your ability. The present moment is the most important focus of your attention, and maintaining that focus is a skill that you can develop. The first step is to become aware of the conversation going on inside your head: what you are saying to yourself and how you are answering your own questions. Sport psychologists call this conversation "self-talk." It is very important to make it productive and useful, and to use it to maintain a focus of attention in the present and on the task.

What are you saying to yourself? Tune in to the conversation going on inside your head. Most people are very undisciplined and let the internal "critic-skeptic" get away with saying things they wouldn't allow anyone else to say. The first thing to listen to is the verb tense being used. Are you talking to yourself about what happened yesterday, or the last time you tried to ski this trail? Are you saying things like "If you fall here, you will . . . ?" To be sure, there is information to be got from past experiences, and there is merit to thinking ahead, but most self-talk about the past and the future is negative and takes your attention away from the challenge in front of you. Focus the conversation on the present and on the things you intend to do. Avoid dwelling on the things you don't want to do.

In addition to maintaining a focus in the present, make the conversation in your head focus on useful instructions. Negative self-talk ("Don't cross your tips, dummy") and the silly, overly positive self-talk that is sometimes recommended ("I'm a great skier, I'm a great skier, I can do it, I can do it . . .") simply don't provide a useful focus of attention or instructions you can translate into effective movement. Self-talk that is nonemotional, not designed to scare you or to fill you with false confidence, and that reminds you of what *to* do, will help you to maintain your focus on the present and on the task, not on the distractions. For example, if you come to a part of a trail that is a bit steeper, it is not effective to say, "Oh . . . , I always fall where it's steep, and I'll slide a long way!" It is more effective to recognize the challenge and give yourself the following useful, but simple tip: "This is a little steeper—finish each turn with your skis across the hill to control your speed." Note that it is important to have some idea about what to do, what the effective skiing maneuvers are in a given situation. Chapters V and VI will help with that, as will a lesson with a qualified instructor. Then it is up to you to translate that information into things you can say to yourself that will keep your attention on your skiing.

The searchlight. There is another metaphor for attention that some athletes find helpful and that we find especially useful for skiers. Think of your attention as a searchlight, one that can be focused narrowly to illuminate a small area brightly, or broadly to see a large area in less detail. When you are about to ski a particular slope, focus the searchlight of your attention on the terrain you are going to ski. Narrow the focus so that distractions such as other skiers, people on the chairlift, the icy access road to the ski area, or the long drive home are not illuminated by the beam of your attention. When your attention is appropriately focused, it is much easier to regulate your self-talk and to emphasize useful self-direction.

Using your attention like a searchlight and regulating your self-talk are components of the skill of keeping your attention on the task. Attentional focus can be developed with practice, and we recommend that you spend some time and effort on doing so. It is a skill we believe will help you ski at your best consistently, and that we think is much more attainable than trying to find "the zone."

Developing Confidence

The second important component of peak performance is a sense of confidence in your ability. Confidence is often confused with other things, such as "positive thinking," or bravado, or cockiness. One aspect of confidence is the assessment you make of how likely it is that you will be able to perform a certain action. Are you able to make a series of solid turns in a foot of new snow all the time, most of the time, every once in a while, or almost never? The second aspect of confidence is whether you believe that the level of skill you can bring to bear on a given situation is sufficient for success. "Can I ski the bumps well enough to try the middle section of Al's Run at Taos?" Perhaps an analogy will help. Think about your skiing skills as a set of tools. The first aspect of confidence is your assessment of how well and consistently you can use the tools in your toolbox. The second aspect of confidence is your assessment of whether your tools are adequate for the job. These assessments are based on your experiences and on information you can obtain from knowledgeable sources, such as a qualified instructor. These aspects of confidence are not completely independent of each other, but it is useful to think of them separately as you develop confidence in your ability as a skier.

The spiral of confidence and performance. The implication of what we have just said is that a sense of confidence depends on a realistic appraisal of your abilities and of the challenges you face. The problem is that confidence and performance operate as a cause-and-effect spiral that goes either up or down. A good performance will cause your confidence to increase, and an increase in confidence will improve performance. But a downward spiral can result either from a decrease in performance or a lack of confidence. Another problem is that changes in confidence seem to be much greater than a given change in performance warrants. One fall in the powder and confidence is shaken so that performance spirals downward. And sometimes one successful run in the bumps leads the skier to attempt to ski terrain that is much too difficult. Confidence must be tied to realistic assessments of ability and challenge, and ability must be developed as the basis of the confidence to try new challenges.

Develop your skills in safe places. The best place to develop your ability is in terrain that you are confident you can handle. Choose terrain that is not threatening, given your current level of ability, for learning and practicing new skills. That is, develop confidence in being able to consistently perform a certain action or maneuver on skis while you are in a situation where the other aspect of confidence, your ability to handle the terrain, can be taken for granted. When a new skill can be performed consistently on terrain that is easy for you, you are ready to begin using that skill to meet new challenges.

Expanding the performance envelope. Many, many skiers have had their confidence destroyed by attempting terrain that was too difficult for them given the tools they had available. A new skill is a fragile tool. If it is used in too difficult a situation it breaks down, fails; and the skier's confidence is undermined. It is important to move gradually into new challenges. Try to ignore the pleas of friends who say, "You can ski it; I know you can." And try to be realistic about your assessment of the match between your new skills and that run you have always wanted to try. You can keep the confidence-performance spiral moving steadily upward if you set realistic, gradually more difficult goals for yourself.

Those big breakthroughs. Sometimes we hear people say something like, "Today was a great breakthrough for me; I was finally able to link my turns smoothly on Powderhorn." You may have made a similar comment at some point in your skiing experience. We believe that what are perceived and remembered as big breakthroughs are really products of skill development and the upward spiral of confidence and performance. There comes a day, or a run, when you finally say, "I've got it!" It can seem like a sudden event, and the pleasure you take from it is one of the rewards of skiing. We see these changes in skiing ability and the development of confidence about previously intimidating terrain in our students and in our own skiing. But we are convinced that this experience is much more frequent when there has been a foundation of skill development and an application of those skills in gradually more difficult terrain.

How do you ski consistently at or near your best, given the distractions and difficulties of skiing? Peak performance depends on both physical and psychological skills. You must develop the ability to use your skis and boots to perform the maneuvers of modern skiing. Learn new skills in safe places and gradually move them into new challenges. Your confidence will grow along with your physical abilities. You must also develop the psychological skill of effectively focusing your attention on the skiing challenge you face. The upcoming chapters are designed to help you acquire the mental and physical skills you need for modern skiing.

Relaxation Techniques

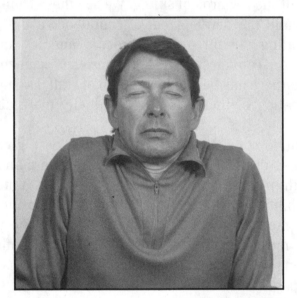

Skiing creates stress; some would even say anxiety; and a few would use words like "fear," "terror," or "panic." To ski well in challenging conditions the stress inherent in skiing must be managed effectively. The finely coordinated movement patterns that you will learn by using this book, by practicing on the snow, and by taking lessons can be disrupted by stress to the extent that you revert to inefficient "survival" skiing. Most skiers have had the experience of "losing it" in the steeps, in the bumps, in heavy crud, on ice, or anywhere that the challenge creates increased stress and tension. There are two ways to deal with this problem. One is "practice, practice, practice!" The more thoroughly a skill has been learned, the less it is affected by stress and anxiety. The other way to deal with stress—and it is a complementary technique, not a substitute for practice—is to learn to relax in the stressful situation. Relaxation does two things for you. First, the physical sensation of tight muscles and jerky movements is eliminated, and it becomes possible to make smooth, powerful, effective movements. Second, muscular relaxation is incompatible with the psychological experience of anxiety. It is just not possible for most humans to feel relaxed and anxious at the same time. We will introduce you to some important relaxation skills in just a bit, but first we want to explain why practice is so important.

PRACTICED PERFECTION

You probably remember taking lessons in music, dance, gymnastics, or some other skilled activity when you were a child. Parents love to shower children with these "advantages." Taking lessons was bad enough, but there was always something worse—it was called a recital. About every six months (it seemed like every other week) you would have to learn a piece of music or a new routine and perform it in front of your parents, everybody else's parents, and, if you were really unlucky, your brothers and sisters. So you would work at learning the new piece and you would finally be able to play it or perform it with only a couple of mistakes, and sometimes not even a single one. Then would come recital night. Clinker after clinker would come bursting forth from your fingers or feet. Why? Because the recital created a level of stress much greater than you experienced in your practice sessions, and the newly learned skills crumbled under the burden. How, then, did the late Vladimir Horowitz give his best performance under the stress of a Carnegie Hall concert appearance or, to get back to skiing, how do Vreni Schneider, Debbie Armstrong, Alberto Tomba, Phil and Steve Mahre, Ingemar Stenmark, and the rest of the skiers who perform so superbly under pressure manage to do their best rather than their worst when an important race is on the line? One part of the answer is simply that they have practiced those skills so many times that no matter how great the pressure or the challenge, a smooth, effective performance is the thing most likely to happen. So, we can immediately prescribe "practice, practice, practice," as one of the important parts of developing pressure-proof technique. We know this is tough medicine, but there is just no way around it. You have to ski, and the more, the better! However, you must practice effective movement patterns; otherwise you are only over-learning errors and making them harder to correct. We will devote much of this book to identifying the fundamental movement patterns of modern skiing and using imagery, indoor practice, and on-the-hill experience to make them the foundation of your own skiing.

RELAXED PERFECTION

Good practice makes your skills more durable under stress; in a complementary way, reducing stress allows you to apply your skills more effectively, even while they are still being learned. Relaxation techniques are among the most effective tools available for the management of stress and anxiety. Psychotherapists use relaxation training to combat anxiety in some of their most difficult cases, such as in dealing with snake phobias. The top performers in athletics, the performing arts, and, yes, even business and government use relaxation techniques to deal with the stress of performing under pressure. There is an additional, important benefit to relaxation training. Visual and kinesthetic imagery is usually much clearer and more vivid when the body and mind are relaxed and receptive. So by learning an effective relaxation technique you will accomplish at least two important things: You will be able to reduce the stress and anxiety in challenging skiing situations so that your best performance can emerge, and you will be able to experience the kind of high-impact imagery that will enable you to learn new skills for even better skiing.

Relaxation Techniques

Perhaps because our society is fast paced and achievement oriented and creates high levels of stress in even ordinary life activities, we have developed a number of techniques designed to reduce stress by inducing a state of relaxation. Many of these techniques are not suitable for our purposes, even though they induce relaxation, because we need a method that can be applied quickly and effectively, in a variety of settings, and without the need for bulky or inconvenient equipment. Relaxation tapes using music or soothing environmental sounds are too slow and you need a tape player to use them. Biofeedback can be helpful in learning to relax, but it is difficult to transport the equipment to the top of a mogul run, and you need a technician to hook you up. Various forms of meditation are also useful in some situations, but you may not want to take twenty minutes repeating your mantra while standing at the top of an untracked powder run because the run will surely have tracks in it when you finish. The method we favor is called progressive relaxation.

Introduction to progressive relaxation. The technique of progressive relaxation was developed by an American physician, Edmond Jacobsen, over fifty years ago, and has been an enduring component of stress management and anxiety control programs ever since. The basis of progressive relaxation is a training sequence in which a muscle group is voluntarily tensed and then allowed to relax. After being tensed the muscles relax beyond their usual level and you experience a distinctive sensation of being warm, heavy, and loose. In addition to tensing and relaxing the muscle groups of your body, you establish a breathing pattern in which you take deep, even breaths, all the way down to your diaphragm. Then, when you tense a muscle group, you breathe in and hold that breath while you experience the tension and let it build. After a few seconds you breathe out and simultaneously allow the muscles to relax. With practice, the pattern of deep, easy breathing becomes a cue for relaxation and you can release tension quickly and effectively. It is also helpful to have another kind of relaxation cue, such as a word or sound you say to yourself each time you release the tension in a muscle group and breathe out. Short, simple words like "calm," "soft," or "aaahh" work best. When the technique has been well learned, it is possible to reduce tension quickly and effectively in almost any situation by breathing in a deep, easy pattern and saying the cue word to yourself each time you breathe out. You then have a tool for coping with the stresses of challenging skiing and for creating a context in which you can use imagery to learn modern ski technique.

On pages 52–59 you'll find a program for learning progressive relaxation. It is a fairly simple one, using only eight muscle groups. It is our experience that athletes and active people can learn the technique well after about five sessions of the full procedure. When you are able to attain a deep sense of relaxation easily using the complete program, you can begin to experiment with using just breathing and the cue word to reduce tension. With practice, you should be able to get almost as relaxed with this abbreviated version as when you use the entire procedure. However, it is important to keep your skills honed by practicing the procedure in its entirety once a week.

SKIER'S GUIDE TO RELAXATION TRAINING

The first step in mental conditioning for peak performance in skiing and other activities is to learn to relax the body deeply, quickly, and whenever desired. Follow the procedure outlined below, which works for most people.

1. Find a comfortable position lying on your back on a mat or sitting in a padded chair.

2. Begin by taking a few deep breaths, breathing all the way down to your diaphragm and breathing out completely.

3. Choose a word that will be your cue to relax. It should be a short word that has a relaxing connotation. "One," "calm," "loose," and "smooth" are all good words to use, but pick a word that has a soothing effect on you.

4. The basic technique is to tense, hold, and then relax the various muscle groups in your body. As you tense your muscles, breathe in, and as you let them relax, breathe out and say the cue word to yourself. As you relax each muscle group notice the difference between the feeling of relaxation and the feeling of tension. You can go through the muscle groups in any order; you may enjoy changing the order or reversing it sometimes. Here are eight muscle groups with suggestions to help you tense and relax them.

FOREHEAD

TENSE: Lift your eyebrows all the way to your hairline.

RELAX: Feel the wrinkles smooth out and the skin flatten.

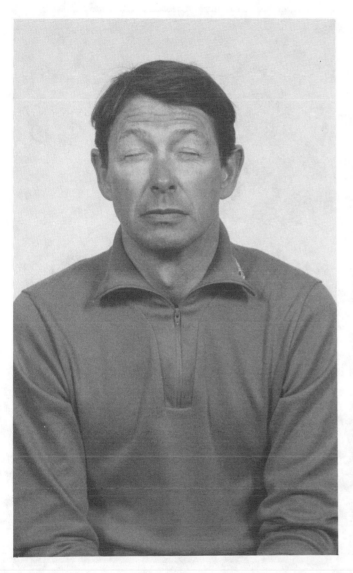 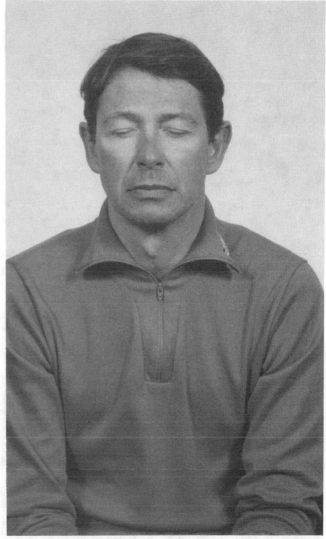

FACE

TENSE: Squeeze your eyes and clench your teeth.

RELAX: Let your eyes almost come open; let your
jaw hang slack and loose.

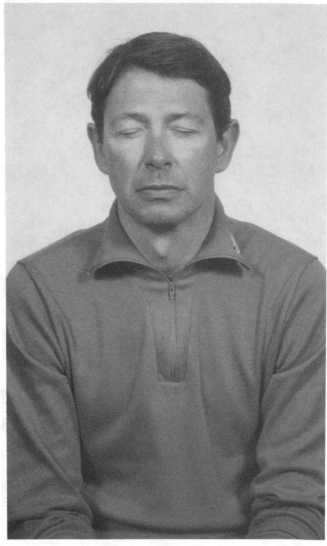

NECK AND
SHOULDERS

TENSE: Lift your shoulders as high as they will go toward your ears.

RELAX: Let your shoulders drop as though your arms were very heavy.

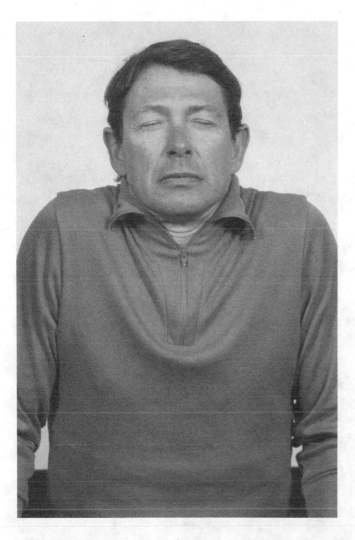
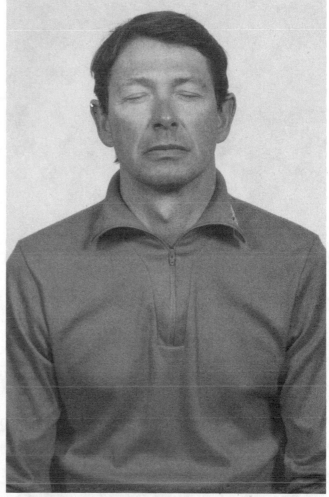

UPPER ARMS, CHEST, AND BACK

TENSE: Bend your arms at the elbow and flex your biceps; squeeze your upper arms against your body.

RELAX: Let your arms fall slack, away from your body; feel your upper body sink into the mat or chair.

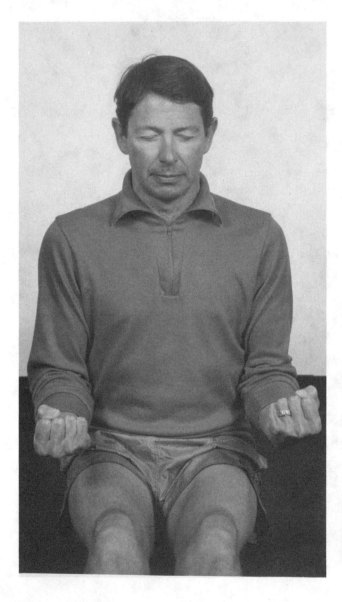

STOMACH

TENSE: Imagine that you are trying to do a sit-up but your feet and head are being held down.

RELAX: Let your stomach muscles fall toward your backbone.

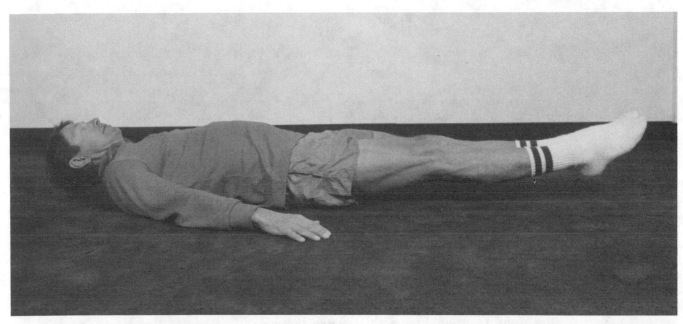

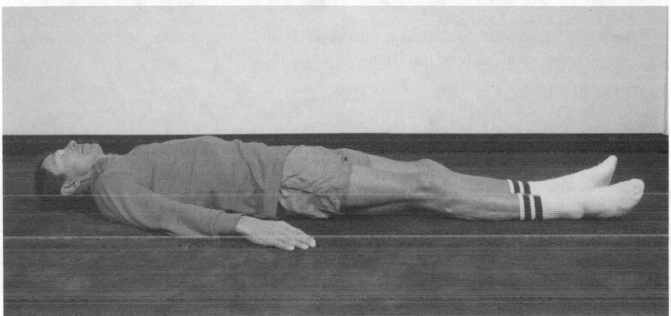

BUTTOCKS

TENSE: Raise yourself up off the mat or the chair just by tightening your buttocks.

RELAX: Let yourself go flat against the mat or the chair.

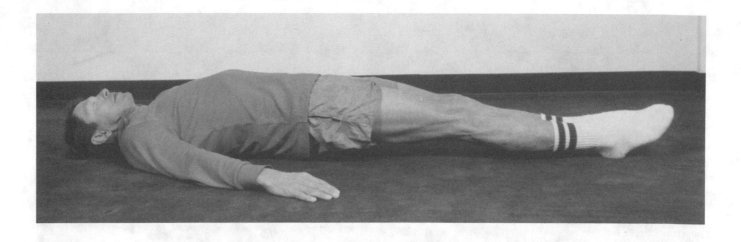

THIGHS
AND SHINS

TENSE: Extend your legs so your knees lock, and flex your toes so they point toward your head.

RELAX: Let your feet fall toward the outside; let your knees bend just a little.

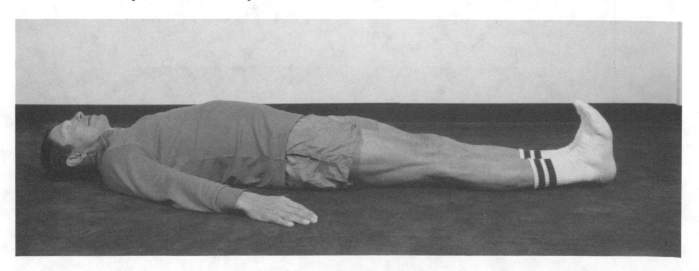

FEET AND
CALVES

TENSE: Point your toes and then curl them as though you were trying with your feet to hold onto a ball.

RELAX: Let go of the ball, then let your feet fall toward the outside.

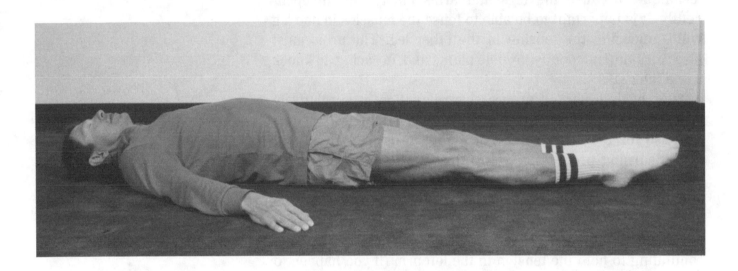

Practice this basic technique until it seems very easy, always remembering to breathe out and to say your cue word as you let each muscle group relax. When you have gone through the eight muscle groups, check for any remaining tension and remove it by tensing and then relaxing the muscles involved. Pay attention to the feeling of relaxation you have after you have gone through the entire procedure.

5. When you have mastered Step 4, see how relaxed you can get just by tensing your whole body a bit while you take a breath and hold it, and then breathing out while saying the cue word, and letting the tension flow out. Check for any tension in specific areas and focus on those, one at a time, while you breathe and say the cue word to yourself. With some practice, you will be able to attain a state of relaxation in only a minute or two, and perhaps even more quickly, by breathing deeply and saying the cue word to yourself as you breathe out.

6. Once a week, repeat the basic technique in Step 4 so that your relaxation skills remain at a high level.

Differential Relaxation

When you have developed the ability to relax deeply and can achieve a state of relaxation quickly and easily using your breathing pattern and cue word, it is time to learn to maintain tension in some muscles while relaxing others. This skill, called differential relaxation, is critical for using modern ski technique, because the legs and arms must work independently. It is important to be able to tense the muscles in one leg while releasing the tension in the other leg. The arms must also work independently for pole plants and, in racing, to knock aside the gates.

After having learned progressive relaxation, it is relatively easy to learn differential relaxation. We'll start with some exercise for the arms. First, tense both arms just as you did while learning progressive relaxation: bend your arms at the elbow, clench your fists, and flex your biceps. The only difference is that we don't want you to squeeze your upper arms against your chest. Now, tense both arms and hold the tension for about ten seconds. Then let the right arm relax while continuing to hold the tension in the left arm (if you happen to be left-handed, just reverse this pattern). Pay attention to the different sensations in your two arms, and notice that it is difficult to let all the tension go in one arm while holding tension in the other. Repeat this exercise five times. Then reverse sides, holding tension in the right arm while releasing tension in the left arm. Again, repeat the exercise five times.

Start the second exercise with your hands at your sides and with very little tension in either arm. Bring your right arm into the tensed position described in the first exercise without moving or increasing the tension in your left arm. Hold the tension in your right arm for ten seconds, and then let it go. Once again, pay attention to the different sensations in your two arms as one is tensed and the other relaxed. Repeat this exercise five times with each arm.

The third exercise is designed to help you learn to pass the tension from arm to arm in a quick, precise pattern. Start with both arms bent at the elbow and your hands in about the position you would hold them to grasp your ski poles. Now tense the right hand, forearm, and upper arm while leaving only enough tension in the left arm to hold it in position. Make your right arm and hand firm and strong, but not rigid. Then release the tension and, almost as if you were passing it from hand to hand, pick it up with your left hand and arm. Start this exercise by holding the tension in each hand for five seconds. When you can pass the tension quickly and smoothly from hand to hand, begin to shorten the interval to, say, three seconds, and then to one second of tension on each side. People who can hand-milk cows and goats will find this exercise easy to master. Be sure that you feel tension through your whole arm, even when the change from hand to hand is very quick. You will need the strength of your whole arm for pole plants in demanding terrain.

The exercises just described will be very useful in developing independent pole action and the quickness needed to deal with choppy bumps or any situation calling for a rapid pattern of turns. However, it is even more important to develop the ability to use your legs independently, in order to apply pressure to one ski at a time by tensing or tightening that leg. The exercises that follow are very similar to the ones we just described for your arms, but you may find them more difficult to do. It is harder for most people to develop differential relaxation in the larger muscles of the lower body. Yet we practice this every day just by walking naturally. First, lie down on your back with your arms at your sides and your legs slightly bent, with heels resting on the floor. Now tense both legs and hold the tension for ten seconds. Then allow your right leg to relax while continuing to hold the tension in your left leg. Again, notice the difference in the sensations in the two legs. After another ten seconds let the tension go from your left leg as well. Repeat this five times, and then switch legs so that you let your left leg relax while your right leg remains tense.

The second exercise is done in the same position: lying down with your legs slightly bent and heels on the floor. Start by letting all the tension go from both legs. Then tense just your right leg without letting any tension develop in your left leg. Hold the tension for ten seconds, and then let it go. Notice again the different sensations in your two legs, and that it is difficult to tense one leg without some tension developing in the other. Repeat this exercise five times for each leg.

Start the third exercise for differential relaxation of the legs in a standing position, with knees slightly bent and your weight balanced on both feet. Now simply pick up your left foot and balance on your right foot. Allow your right leg to support you while the left leg is relaxed. Hold just enough tension in your left leg to keep it up off the floor. Notice the different sensations in the two legs—the right should be tense, but not rigid, while the left should be relaxed but ready to support you if needed. Balance on your right foot at least ten seconds, long enough to really feel the different sensations in the two legs. Then put both feet on the floor, balance evenly for a moment, and pick up your right foot and let your left leg support you. Again, pay attention to the different sensations in your two legs. Repeat this exercise several times with both legs so that you really become familiar with the sensations. The next step is to begin to move the tension from foot to foot with a quick but precise change. This is not hopping! While standing on your right foot, put the left foot down and tense the left leg so it will hold your weight; *then* pick up the right foot. After you have transferred your weight, stay on your left foot long enough to feel the different sensations once again. After the weight transfer becomes easy to do, you can begin to shorten the length of time you remain on each foot to five seconds, then to three, and finally to one second. Remember, even when you are moving quickly from foot to foot, this is not an exercise in hopping. The weight transfer should be smooth, with a noticeable difference in tension between the weighted and unweighted legs. The ability to transfer your weight from foot to foot is a natural extension of the ability to tense one leg while allowing the other to relax, and is one of the keys to modern ski technique.

Uses and Abuses of Relaxation

One of the ways to use progressive relaxation is to provide a context for the use of imagery when visualizing yourself in action. Imagery is more vivid and effective, and the sense of movement is much stronger, if your body is relaxed and your mind is focused. The athletes at Arizona State University who participate in the Applied Sport Psychology Program learn progressive relaxation and then, while deeply relaxed, focus on images of perfect performance or on images of new skills. You'll be introduced to those imagery techniques in Chapter IV, and you'll use them in Chapter V to learn the movement patterns of modern ski technique. But remember that a well-developed relaxation skill is a critical part of using imagery effectively.

The other major use of relaxation techniques in skiing, other sports, and life is to reduce stress so that you can perform at your best. But it is important to realize that just being relaxed is not enough to produce a great run in the bumps, in the powder, or in the gates. You will need to be able to adjust your relaxation and arousal to the level that allows you to perform at your optimum level. If you're too relaxed you're sluggish, slow, and lack enthusiasm and power. If you're too tense you're twitchy, jumpy, and unable to control the fine movements required for really high-performance skiing. How do you find the level that is right for you? You have to experiment with it after you have learned an effective relaxation skill.

Our experience is that most people are too tense most of the time while they ski, so you can start from the premise that you will want to calm down rather than "psych up." However, things can work differently. Some skiers have a bad habit of nearly going to sleep in the middle of a run. They start out fine, hit the first turn and then the second, get a good rhythm—and then in the middle of the pitch get so mellow and relaxed that any change in the terrain knocks them off balance and out of control for the rest of the run. You can do a bit of self-diagnosis to find out whether you need to be more relaxed or more alert. Too much tension feels like a small electric shock is hitting you almost constantly; fine movements are difficult to control, and you spend a lot of time going back and forth to the restroom. Being too relaxed feels like somebody put your whole life in slow motion; you're late for everything, and you don't really care. Being at the right level usually gives you a sense of being in control, focused on the task, confident, and having plenty of time to do what you have to do. It feels great.

There is another very important ingredient in peak performance. You have to have the skills needed to perform the actions that are required. It isn't much help to be able to relax at the top of a steep bump run if you don't have a clue as to how to ski the bumps, or the powder, or the crud, or in the trees, or through the gates. "Relax and just let it happen" is a good way to get to know your area's Ski Patrol and to have the toboggan ride of your life. When you can take control of your level of arousal and adjust the tension level in your body to its optimum point, you must then be able to call out of your memory the skilled movement patterns you need to ski the terrain in front of you. You must give yourself positive instructions about things *to* do, not negative instructions about how not to ski. There is a big difference between saying to yourself, "Don't sit back, dummy!" and saying, "Balance on the sweet spot; move from foot to foot." In some instances it is important to focus on sound fundamental, movement patterns, like the balance and movement statement just above. In other instances the focus may be more specific; the timing of pole plants, for example.

Sometimes terrain and conditions call for a specific tactical approach to the pitch you are about to ski. In heavy, cut-up crud, for example, it is a good tactic to ski a little faster, to be patient enough to ski a longer-radius turn and finish it across the hill for a bit of speed control, and to tip the ski a bit more on its edge so it slices through the crud. At the top of a crud pitch, use your relaxation technique to get to your optimum level of arousal, and then focus on the skiing task with a simple, positive self-instruction like, "Longer, rounder; carry some speed into the next turn." Notice that it is difficult to put into words all the components you might want to include. This is where the imagery skills you will learn in the next chapter become valuable tools in everyday skiing, not just techniques you employ only when you are learning a new skill. When your ability to use imagery has developed to high level, you will be able to use it in combination with relaxation to ski a particular run just the way you want. You can take the image of an instructor demonstrating how to ski the crud, or you can take the self-instructional statement we used above, and translate either of them into an image—an image that you can also feel. Then, alert and relaxed, you can ski with that feeling, ski yourself into that image, with a heightened sense of power and control that makes skiing the natural high we all love.

Imagery for Better Skiing

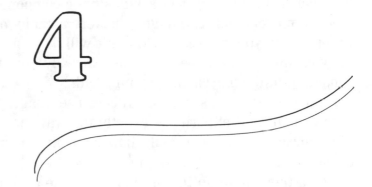

4

The words "imagery" and "visualization" have been used in many different ways in books and articles on learning and peak performance in sports. We intend to use these words interchangeably to mean a specific kind of mental representation of physical activity. For us, imagery is a process of experiencing yourself in a specific situation and, in your mind, seeing, hearing, and feeling yourself move in that place. Imagery may also include smelling, tasting, and touching in order to create as much impact as possible. In this book we will show how to use imagery to extend the learning process to include the experience of skiing with movement patterns fundamental to modern ski technique. When you develop good imagery skills, you can take the movements you are learning out of your living room and onto the ski slopes, even if it is July in Manhattan, not February in Taos. The payoff, in addition to the fun of imagining that you are skiing while it is really ninety-five in the shade, is that you will accelerate the rate at which you learn to apply your new moves on real snow. You can practice the skills you are trying to learn over and over again, perfectly, in your mind. And because good imagery has a kinesthetic component, you will feel the movements as though you were actually on the snow. Later, when you are really skiing, it will be easier to perform as you intend, because you have already experienced the sensation of the movement in your head.

Most of the world's best ski racers use imagery before the race to plan and experience exactly the way they want to ski the course. This is especially important in slalom races, because competitors cannot ski the course before the actual race. Instead, they climb up the hill alongside the course and memorize the pattern of gates. If you watch them closely, you'll see them stop and, sometimes, close their eyes, and with their hands or by making small movements with the lower body pretend to ski a series of gates. Just before being called to the starting gate you will see them do the same thing. Their imagery skills are so well honed that they know what the course will feel like before they get on it, and that image becomes a template guiding their movements when they push out of the starting gate. In a similar fashion, you can use imagery to design a series of turns that embody the new skills you are learning. You can start that process while you are in your living room, and you can continue it as you look down at untracked powder, a bump run, or a groomed slope that you want to ski well.

IMAGES, METAPHORS, AND NONSENSE

Imagery is a powerful tool for learning and growth in many different areas of our lives. But it has also been the focus of a lot of nonsense about how people can learn new skills and make changes in their lives. There are many books and videos available that imply that if you can visualize something, you can have it; a new job, a new car, a new skill, a new lover. We don't think it is that simple. Imagery *is* a powerful tool, but in order to make changes in the way you ski or the way you live your life, you have to do more than just think about it. So in this book we will combine imagery with indoor exercises and on-the-slope drills to help you learn the movement patterns of modern skiing.

There is often some confusion about the difference between imagery and the use of metaphors and similes. Metaphors and similes are very useful parts of our language, and descriptions of ski technique abound in them. Joubert was a master at choosing the right word, in French, to convey the feeling of a movement pattern. *Avalement* (swallowing) was his description of a skier's absorbing the undulations in terrain such as a field of moguls. "Surf technique" described the act of pushing the skis laterally to the outside of a turn. Many ski instructors use figures of speech to convey movement patterns because a well-chosen phrase can communicate in a few seconds what would otherwise take many words of kinesthetic jargon. But the danger in this practice is using metaphors and similes that simply don't describe an effective movement pattern. For example, we could tell you to ski "like a panther that is chasing a deer." "Wow," you might say, "these guys have got some great images!" Nonsense! That's not an image, at least not the kind you will be using to learn modern ski technique. It's a figure of speech, and for some people it might translate into a movement pattern that would be effective in their skiing. But, for others, the response might well be a baffled "What?" And the impact on their skiing would be nil, or even negative.

Let's take another example. We know a former instructor who was fond of using color as a metaphor for skiing. One of his favorite instructional techniques was to tell his students to "Ski your favorite color!" Often this instruction was given without being accompanied by more practical advice on how to turn and stop. Not many students found that skiing their favorite color translated into accomplishment on skis, and they told this to the ski school director. The instructor found another line of work. "OK," you say, "color is not a good metaphor." Well, it *can* be. Another instructor we know, Scott Goeller, used color brilliantly in a lesson he told us about. He was skiing with a woman artist who was just not taking charge of the skis at the end of her turns and, as a result, was getting knocked around by every little bump and rut on the mountain. Scott asked her to name the most passionate color she used in her painting. "Purple," she said. "Great," said Scott. "Add a little purple to the end of each turn." She did, and she began to ski more powerfully, and was more in charge of what was happening to her skis. Why did it work for Scott and not for our other friend? Because it was the right figure of speech for the right person at the right time. In this case it was a stroke of genius. These figures of speech work, however, only if the words translate into movement, and in our case, only if the words translate into effective movement patterns for modern skiing. We will try to be very careful using figures of speech in this book, because we can't be sure that each of you will attach the same meaning as we do to "ski like a hungry coyote."

There is another way some ski instructors and other gurus attempt to convey the feeling of a new skill. They try to evoke a feeling you may have had in another sport or activity by saying, "It feels just like . . ." The last word of the sentence could describe anything from bowling to sex, depending on the kind of experiences the guru has had. Our experience tells us that skiing *isn't* "just like" anything else. As we said earlier, there are many reasons to consider skiing an unnatural act. Sliding downhill at a fairly high rate of speed on a pair of slippery boards is likely to trigger a number of very human reactions, most of which are not useful if you want to ski well. Getting the skis to take you where you want to go at the rate of speed you want to get there requires movement patterns that are not "just like" anything else you do. So, we don't agree that shifting weight from ski to ski is just like riding a bicycle. (Actually, the bicycle analogy is one of the better ones, and riding a bike *is* good strength training for your legs, but the actual movements used in skiing are very different from those used pedaling a bike.)

In a few instances, there is a nearly universal understanding of how to translate a phrase into a change in how you ski. We find that a lot of people who are skiing defensively adopt a position that includes a protruding posterior. Many of them find a more functional stance when we tell them to "make a somewhat suggestive forward movement of the hips." Some of you will recognize that as a description of what burlesque dancers do, as in "————and grind." Some of the other sport and movement analogies are much less useful, but we have heard everything from bowling to dart throwing touted as being just like skiing.

One skill that does transfer from sport to sport is good balance. But even here, the balance you need to use your skis effectively to make turns is a bit different from the balance you need to receive a serve in tennis, to play defense in basketball, or to hit a golf ball. One of the first things we'll ask you to do in Chapter V is to find the balance that is most effective for skiing and, as you'll see, it will be different from the balance you use in other activities.

We don't intend all of this to mean that nothing you have done in the past will be useful as you try to change your skiing. Anything you have done to develop your ability to move with strength and precision, as well as the increased kinesthetic sensitivity you have gained so that you are aware of your movements and can guide them effectively, will be helpful as you learn the movement patterns of modern skiing. But the transfer from other activities is not a direct or specific one, so the images we will help you develop will not depend on movements that are "just like" those in some other sport. Our imagery and exercises and drills will be focused directly on what will help you ski.

Imagery Is a Skill

Imagery is most vivid and effective when the mind and body are relaxed and able to focus on the images and experience the movements in them. Therefore, the first step, and one that we hope you have already taken, is to learn an effective relaxation technique. Whenever you have attained a state of deep relaxation, you can begin or continue to develop your imagery skills. We teach imagery and relaxation skills almost simultaneously when we lead indoor sessions. The first training session for relaxation is followed immediately, while the students are still deeply relaxed, with an introductory session on imagery.

As with any other skill, imagery develops from the easily mastered to the more difficult, so we usually start with an easy task like bringing into focus an image of a familiar room or outdoor location. Imagery skills are developed by focusing on the details of the scene; don't be satisfied with a loose approximation. The image's impact is enhanced by engaging as many of the senses as possible. See the image, but also hear the music, smell the roses, and touch the thorns. When you work on skiing imagery, see the snow, the trees, the other skiers, and the bumps, and hear the skis on the snow, feel the cold air on your face, smell the pine trees, and feel your body move as you ski.

A training program for developing your imagery skills is presented on pages 70–78. If you work through that sequence and have an imagery session immediately after each relaxation training session, in a short time you'll have both of these important skills available to help you become a better skier.

A GUIDE TO IMAGERY SKILLS

The second tool to be used in mental training for peak performance in skiing and for accelerating the rate at which you learn new movement patterns is the creation of vivid mental images so that desired skills can be rehearsed in imagery before you are actually on the slopes. Some people seem to create images very easily; others have more difficulty, but with practice almost everyone can learn this skill. The following procedure can be used by anyone. Even if you find it easy to create images, working through this procedure will help you sharpen them and make them more useful.

1. Find a comfortable position on a mat or in a padded chair away from loud noises and bright lights.

2. Relax. Using the relaxation technique described in Chapter III, reach a state of deep relaxation.

3. Start by trying to visualize a familiar place, one where you like to be. Try to see as many details as possible, and see how clear you can make the picture become. Involve all your senses. See the shapes, colors, and textures; feel the surfaces, smell the air, hear the noises, taste the wind. Be as fully present in your imagined place as possible. If you are distracted or your mind wanders, don't fight it; instead take a few deep breaths and repeat your relaxation cue, then focus on the image again.

4. Now slowly scan the whole scene, paying attention to how clear the image is. Rate it on this scale.

      5 = Very clear, like a good photograph
      4 = Fairly clear; a little out of focus
      3 = Blurry; hard to make out details
      2 = Very blurry; hard to tell what the picture is
      1 = No image at all

Rating your images regularly will help you develop imaging skills.

5. When you can attain a clear image of a familiar place (a number 4 or 5 on the scale), practice letting it go out of focus, to a 1, and then bringing it back. It may help to imagine that you are focusing a camera, turning the focusing ring until the picture is very clear.

6. Now practice focusing and unfocusing images of a variety of familiar objects and places. Keep practicing until it is easy for you to create number 4 and 5-quality images. Begin to include ski equipment in your imagery. It is helpful to use a ski poster as a target image, but be sure to get a recent one of a great skier, say, Phil or Steve Mahre, Debbie Armstrong, or any other of the recent World Cup or Olympic champions. If you are going to spend a lot of time looking at a poster, both directly and in your imagery, we want it to give you the image of modern skiing. Check your images by rating them and by comparing the image to the actual piece of equipment or to the poster. Concentrate on details of texture, markings, and logos. Remember to relax while you use imagery.

Going Skiing in Your Mind

The next step in developing your imagery skills is to learn to visualize yourself actually skiing. Start, as with any imagery session, by finding a quiet place, and then use your relaxation technique to attain a deeply relaxed state. Follow the suggestions offered below. As soon as each step can be accomplished easily, with clear images, move on to the next.

Just like being there. Get into your ski boots. Buckle 'em up snugly; there's no reason we can't put a little reality into your imagery. Now put on your ski gloves and pick up your ski poles. We don't think you need to put on a hat and goggles, but if this helps, go ahead! Now, before you go any further, pay attention to the sensation—the feel—of your ski gear. Notice the snugness of the boots, the sense of support and pressure against your shins. Notice the feel of the poles in your hands; their weight, the balance as you swing them. Flex your knees and ankles slightly so that you feel solidly balanced on the arches of your feet, a little bit toward the heel. Move up and down a little, and rock back and forth until you feel balanced and centered. Now relax. Breathe in and out, deeply, in a slow rhythm, and silently repeat your relaxation cue word. We want you to be able to imagine you are about to start skiing, and to be relaxed, not tense.

On your skis, on the snow. Now imagine that you are nearly ready to start. For this session, have your boots on and your ski poles nearby. Check your level of relaxation. If you have started to tense up or to breathe more quickly and shallowly, just take several deep, slow breaths, and repeat your cue word to yourself each time you breathe out. Now, close your eyes and let an image of walking in your boots from the lodge to where you have left your skis form. Check to determine if you are seeing yourself from the outside, as though you are watching a videotape, or if you are seeing from the inside, as though you are actually walking. Try both ways, and see which way gives you the clearer image or feels more natural. Use the outside or the inside image, whichever feels better to you, in the following steps. Feel the snow crunch under your boots as you walk, and feel yourself rock from heel to toe as you walk in the boots. Experience finding your skis and laying them out on the snow. Cock the bindings if needed. Then experience yourself knocking the snow off the bottom of your boots, one boot at a time, and stepping into the bindings. Feel the pressure as you push down on the heel piece, and hear the "click" as the binding snaps into place. (You may want to lay your skis out on the floor and actually get into the bindings, to remind yourself of all the steps and their sensations. Go through the real process several times, and then re-create it with imagery. You will soon be able to have an imagery experience that is nearly as vivid as the real action. Pay special attention to the sensations of motion and muscle action. Creating vivid experiences of motion in your mind will help you move toward the "image" of modern skiing while you are still in your living room.)

When you are able to experience yourself going through the process of putting on your skis in a vivid way, feeling the movements you go through without actually moving at all, it is time to extend your imagery to include movements you can't make in your living room. So, go through the process of getting into your skis, using your boots, gloves, and poles as props to help you get a vivid, kinesthetic (muscle movement) image. You could even click into your bindings the first few times you do this exercise to help you get a really strong image. Now, without actually moving, experience yourself sliding your skis back and forth on the snow, just the way you would after you put them on to check to see that they have a nice, smooth gliding action. Feel the skis move smoothly over the snow, feel yourself balanced on your poles, step from foot to foot, and feel the movements in your legs as you slide each ski. Remember, you are not really moving during this exercise, just re-creating movement patterns that are already familiar. When the sensation of movement in your legs is very strong, try some changes. What would it feel like if there was some ice on the bottom of your right ski? How would that sensation be different from that of the left ski as it moves smoothly over the snow? Work with this simple movement pattern until you are able experience it realistically, without any props at all. Then you'll be on your way to going skiing in your mind.

For a little change, let's ride a bike. At this point, it may be helpful to shift to another form of motion, such as another athletic activity, to further develop your ability to create kinesthetic images. We like to use a bicycle ride as an imagery practice exercise because it involves muscular movements of the legs that are similar to some aspects of skiing, and because almost everybody rides or has ridden a bike. Again, start by attaining a state of deep relaxation. Then experience yourself outdoors, walking toward your bike, on a nice autumn day. Stop for a moment and check out what you're wearing; see the colors and logos, feel the texture of the cloth against your skin. Now move to your bike, unlock it, and check it out—pinch the tires, spin the crank backwards, test the brake levers. Be sure to see the colors and logos, and to feel your movements as you do all of this. Now swing up onto the bike and start to accelerate smoothly, feeling the muscles in your legs begin to work, feeling the air begin to move against your face. Experience yourself riding down a smooth, uncrowded road, and feel the pleasurable sensations of your muscles working against the load as you pedal faster. Soon you come to a hill, and you feel the pedals get harder to push. You shift down a gear and really begin to work. You slow down, but you feel your legs moving up and down on the pedals as you exert more effort. Finally you are at the top. You straighten up, breathe deeply, and begin to enjoy the cool wind as you coast downhill. Feel the sensations in your legs as they begin to recover from the effort. Then continue to experience yourself coasting on the bike, gradually letting the image fade until you open your eyes and find yourself back in your living room.

Use a bicycle ride, a training run, ice skating, or any other activity that is easy, feels good, and involves using your legs for this exercise. The important thing is to develop your ability to have vivid "body in motion" images. With that ability, you will be able to change your skiing more rapidly and more effectively than you thought possible.

By now you may be thinking, "OK, OK; when do we start working on my skiing?" Patience. Actually, we don't want you to start developing images of your own skiing until you have done some of the drills and exercises in Chapter V. If you have developed good imagery skills, it would be counterproductive to use them to re-create the way you used to ski. Having a vivid imagery session, using your former ski technique is equivalent to going out and practicing the movements you are trying to change. We want you to experience the new movement patterns and get familiar with them, and *then* develop images of yourself skiing using those movements and not the technique you are trying to change.

Imagery for ski fever. We hope that you are reading this book sometime in the early autumn so that you can begin to use it well before the ski season. But we know that skiers get very impatient during October and November, and we know that you will want to think about skiing and even dwell on vivid images of bottomless powder or endless moguls. And we just told you *not* to dwell on images of your former technique. So, what is a skier to do? Well, we think ski fever is great, and we catch a good case of it every fall, too. You can use your imagery skill to have a beneficial case of ski fever if you pick out the right skiers to use as images. Many of the ski movies that come to town, along with the ski shows and the preseason sales, have shots of excellent skiers using modern technique. Ski movies from earlier years are now available on video, and there are many instructional videos with great skiers who use sound technique. It is helpful to shop around a bit to find a movie or a videotape that has footage of the kind of terrain you like to ski, and a skier who is of your gender and about your size. When you find a sequence that seems to be what you want, look at it critically, referring to our discussions and the pictures from the earlier chapters of this book. Be sure that what you are watching is good, modern ski technique, not just a great athlete catching big air and making spectacular recoveries. Now you are ready to catch a truly helpful case of ski fever.

Begin by cueing up the sequence you want to watch on your VCR. Watch it several times, not with a critical eye but with attention to the movement patterns and the rhythms used by the skier. If the sequence includes music that is coordinated with the movements, leave it on. If not, just turn down the sound. Now, use just the breathing and the cue word from your relaxation routine to reduce the level of tension in your body. Then, as you watch, let your body begin to experience the movements you are seeing. If you have skied for a couple of seasons, you'll be able to empathize with the movement patterns of the skiers you are watching. It is helpful to find a segment that has some slow motion footage in it so you can really see what the skiers are doing and begin to translate their movements into your own kinesthetic awareness. After you have watched a segment a few times you'll find that you can replay it on your own as imagery, and that you can experience the feeling of movement while you watch the pictures in your mind.

We must caution you about two things. First, the sense of movement you get from this kind of imagery is not as precise as the specific movement patterns you'll experience by doing the exercises in Chapter V. But if you have chosen your target image well, it will help you make progress toward better skiing. Second, the sense of moving with the skiers on the film can be almost addictive, and the case of ski fever you get by following this exercise will be the almost as intense as the night before the opening day of the new season.

From the picture in your mind to the movement in your feet. How do the pictures in our minds translate into body movements? Scientists who study how we learn and control our movements talk a lot about schemas and motor programs. These are considered to be the codes stored in the brain that are activated in a given situation and that guide the movements we make. There is much disagreement over whether motor programs are like computer programs. Are they initiated by certain instructions and then run off precisely as they were encoded? If this were so, it would mean you would need a different program for every different mogul you ski. Or are movements controlled by more flexible schemas that allow us to accommodate to the unique requirements of each bump we encounter? We don't need to settle the argument here or even to pick sides. It is sufficient to realize that movements are guided by some kind of memory or plan and that, however the plan is created, it can produce the movements we want. Imagery works as a way to learn to ski, or to play tennis, or to dance because the imagery creates a motor program than can be accessed to re-create the movement, sometimes without ever really having done it.

A story is told among sport psychologists about Kurt Thomas, the famous American gymnast. Thomas was attempting to learn a very difficult trick on the horizontal bar. This move involves releasing the bar during a series of giant swings, doing a somersault above the bar, and catching it again on the way down. Thomas rehearsed the trick in his mind literally thousands of times before he actually tried it on the bar. Of course, he was all rigged up with a safety harness, and everyone expected a long process of getting closer and closer before he actually "caught it," as gymnasts say. He did the trick on the first attempt, the story goes, and when asked how he was able to do something so complicated and dangerous the very first time, he said it was easy. "I've been up there above the bar a thousand times *in my mind,* so I knew exactly how it would feel."

How are motor programs transferred from your mind to your muscles? We'll leave the scientists to work that out, but we can be confident that a well-learned image can be translated into movement. Perhaps we can't all do this as quickly as Kurt Thomas or some of the other dazzling athletes we admire, but with some well-focused practice a clear image can certainly be transferred to new movements. To help make the point, try this exercise. On a sheet of 8½″ × 11″ paper, sign your first name in large script, using most of the page. Now put that aside, and take off the shoe and sock of your dominant foot (the one you would use to kick something). Place a pen or pencil between your big toe and your second toe so you can write with your foot. Now put a pad of paper on the floor and try to sign your first name with your foot. The first try will feel very awkward, the second less so; eventually you'll be able to write your name pretty smoothly with your foot. We know this sounds a little silly, but keep at it until you get the hang of it. When you are signing your name with a fairly smooth, coordinated movement, compare the signature you made with your foot to the one you made with your hand a little while ago. The two will probably look a lot alike. If you practice a bit more, trying to get your foot-written signature to look like the handwritten version, you'll see that the resemblance gets closer and closer and that your foot signature includes some of the little peculiarities of your handwriting. Why does this exercise work? Because there is a motor program that generates your signature. It is a very well-learned program; you could think of it as giving rise to a vivid, kinesthetic image that is then able to guide the movement of your foot. The transfer is not immediate and it is not perfect. You will still have to put in a lot of practice in order to be able to sign your name as well with your foot as you do with your hand.

The impact of imagery on your skiing will be much like what happened in this exercise. You probably won't ski exactly like the image you have the first time you try, but the image will guide your practice, the approximations will get closer and closer, and you'll learn a lot faster than you would without the image. Also, because kinesthetic images can be transferred from limb to limb and from hands to feet, you will be able to use your hands to create movement patterns such as the shapes of modern ski turns while you are indoors and transfer them to your feet when you are on the snow.

Ski Just Like the Picture in Your Mind

If you have been working diligently, with time out for a break now and then, you now have the tools to make some changes in your skiing—fundamental changes in the way you use the skis on the snow, not just cosmetic changes that will show off this year's "look." Your skill at relaxation makes it possible for you to put yourself in a psychological state that allows you to create vivid mental images of yourself on skis, including the sensations of muscle movement and of motion. In addition, that relaxation skill will enable you to use new movement patterns more quickly when you really go skiing. When you relax and reduce your level of arousal, you will be able to apply the new skills you will develop in Chapter V, rather than falling back on the old, inefficient patterns because you're nervous. That means you will spend less time practicing old, bad habits and more time practicing and perfecting an exciting new way to ski.

Your skill at imagery will be useful at every point in the process of learning new movement patterns. As you'll see in Chapter V, we will introduce new movements that are the foundation of modern skiing with simple exercises you can do at home. But it will be important to get the right feeling for each movement, and we'll describe that for you in a way that will allow you to create a kinesthetic image before you even begin to move. Then you'll be able to compare your actual movements, experienced through your kinesthetic sense, with the image we have helped you create. So, in a way, you create a template for the right move by developing a vivid image. After you have practiced the fundamental movement pattern and learned to repeat it accurately, we'll introduce some variations and complications that you will need to learn in order to move closer to actual skiing. Again, we will help you develop an image of the movement pattern, and how it feels to do it right, as a template against which to evaluate your practice. The next step will be to combine fundamental movements into the more complex patterns that occur when you are really on the snow. Putting things together to produce the movements of efficient, modern skiing will require that you develop another image, a more elaborate one, as a standard of comparison, while you learn at this new level of organized, coordinated movement.

Finally, it will be an enormous help to practice the new techniques by going skiing in your mind. When you have learned the movements of modern skiing, your ability to create vivid images of faraway places will allow you to practice your new skills on your favorite runs, at your favorite mountain. So, when people ask you, in July, in Manhattan, what you're grinning about, you can say, "I just had a lifetime-best run in the bumps on Al's Run at Taos, truly awesome!"

Kinesthetic Awakening at Home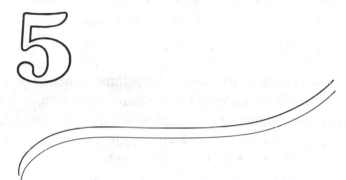

In this chapter we will explore stance and movement patterns associated with balance, through drills and exercises that can be practiced at home. Kinesthetic awareness refers to your ability to perceive the actions of the muscles and joints used in functional skiing. For many, this chapter will represent the heart of the book. Do not, however, forgo the previous chapters on relaxation and imagery. Imagery, in particular, will be utilized in conjunction with the indoor exercises contained in this chapter, and will play an important role in helping you internalize the movement patterns these exercises create.

As with any fundamental skill, it is difficult to practice too much. Furthermore, it is important that you become familiar enough with the movements to recall them in the midst of the distractions of the slope. This chapter in particular might be best utilized if it is reviewed just before hitting the slopes. Ideally, you will read and develop these exercises over the summer, and then go through the exercises again about two weeks prior to the first ski trip of the year. Since this chapter can be reviewed in a few hours, it can be of great value in the autumn, when ski fever peaks. Instead of just dreaming about skiing, you will be able to re-create the motions involved.

THE KID

Previously we spoke of the importance of breathing, balance, and the fundamentals of skiing. Early on, as this book began to take shape and we talked about our approach, we developed a strong sense of déjà vu. Suddenly it clicked: it was the movie *The Karate Kid.* It became our favorite analogy of the learning process we envisioned. For those who have never seen the movie or who have not seen it for a while, here is a brief recap.

It is the story of a teenage boy, Daniel, who is befriended by a handyman. Daniel has just moved with his mother from New Jersey to California and is having difficulty blending in. This difficulty takes the form of being beaten up regularly by a group of teenage delinquent karate students. The handyman, Mr. Miyagi, is of Okinawan descent and has a penchant for bonsai trees. After a number of encounters with the karate students, including Miyagi's rescuing Daniel from another beating, Daniel convinces Miyagi to teach him the secrets of karate. To keep Daniel from getting pummeled while he is in training, Miyagi makes a deal with the gang. If they lay off Daniel for the next two months, Daniel will enter the upcoming karate tournament, and this will be their opportunity to "get" Daniel. Daniel now has a clear goal: to learn enough karate in two months to survive the onslaught of five larger, stronger, more experienced karate students.

Daniel shows up early one Saturday morning to begin his training. He is very excited about getting right into the kicks and punches so that he will soon be able to beat the powder out of the bad guys. Miyagi's first requirement is that Daniel follow his instructions to the letter, without question. After establishing the ground rules, Miyagi gives Daniel his first assignment. He is to wash and wax five antique cars sitting in the backyard. He further instructs Daniel on how he wants each car waxed. With his left hand, Daniel will use counterclockwise strokes to apply the wax. With his right hand, he will remove the wax with clockwise strokes. Miyagi reiterates his instructions visually: "Wax on, wax off." The only other instruction Miyagi gives Daniel is to continue to breathe deeply and regularly, in through the nose and out through the mouth.

Over the course of the next few weeks, Miyagi has Daniel perform a host of chores. They include hand-sanding a huge deck using specific circular motions and painting a fence with long strokes, using the left hand to paint the small boards and the right hand to cover the large boards. Daniel then tackles painting the house using only long, horizontal strokes of the brush. In each case, Miyagi describes specific movements to use to accomplish each task, and reinforces the importance of proper breathing. Confused about the relevance of this whole process, Daniel finally snaps, and demands that Miyagi start teaching him karate rather than having him serve as a domestic worker. In reply Miyagi unleashes a flurry of punches at Daniel. Without missing a beat, Daniel fends off each punch. The movements he has been using for weeks in working around Miyagi's house are precisely the movements required to deflect each blow. Daniel reacted automatically to the punches because he had made each move so many times he was able to draw upon these movements without thinking about them. The impact of what has just happened shakes Daniel, as he recalls all the seemingly useless housework he had done. Now he knows he is learning.

The next part of Daniel's training is to develop balance. Daniel is still eager to get into punching and kicking, but Miyagi again asks for patience. Miyagi emphasizes his point this way: "Balance no good, karate no good. Might as well pack up and go home." So they go to the beach to work on balance. Miyagi has Daniel try to balance on one leg in the surf. While Daniel is being thrashed about in the waves, he sees Miyagi practicing a kick on the beach. Balanced on one foot on top of a piling, arms extended, Miyagi leaps up and fires a kick with the leg which had been on the piling and lands gracefully on his other foot. Daniel is intrigued. This is the type of move he had imagined he would learn. They do not discuss this rather bizarre move, but the next day finds Daniel out at the beach on a piling trying it himself.

The visual impact of this kick on the viewing public was immense. Children everywhere, it seemed, were trying out this move in their living rooms. At age six, Doug's godson, Piper, worked on and perfected this kick using far more determination than with anything previously in his life.

For Daniel, this was also an image with grace and power. His work on balance continued. While Miyagi fished, he had Daniel stand on the bow of his tiny, rather tippy boat and

**Ralph Macchio in *The Karate Kid.*
Courtesy of Columbia Pictures.**

practice defensive hand movements. Then, finally, it was time to punch. Miyagi, dressed like a deranged baseball catcher, has Daniel begin throwing punches. He tells him that the secret to punching is to "drive the whole body into one inch" and "to focus power." Daniel's punches become more and more focused, more and more powerful.

With the training behind them, the day of the tournament is at hand. Daniel is understandably nervous. He does not even know how points are scored toward determining a winner, and his first match is just minutes away. Miyagi soothes him by saying, "Trust the quality of what you know, not the quantity." The outcome? You really should see the movie. Suffice it to say that Daniel has been well prepared for the tournament, and it is a great finale.

All right, what is the connection between *The Karate Kid* and *Visual Skiing*? It's the process. The process begins with a goal: in the movie, survival. To achieve this goal Daniel begins with movement templates ("wax on, wax off"), moves into a program emphasizing balance and then into training to develop the ability to focus power. All these steps are supported by an underpinning of quality breathing. Miyagi asks Daniel to trust the quality of what he knows, not the quantity. It was difficult for Daniel to accept balance and simple movements as the core of karate. It may also be difficult for you to accept balance and simple movements as the basis of effective skiing. You may have a vision of mastering classic technique as your goal, or you may have the idea that skiing is complicated and that you have to have an immense "bag of tricks" to ski well under a variety of conditions. You do not need to know, and indeed you cannot know in advance, the exact movement pattern required for every turn you will make on skis. If you have good balance and your body knows the fundamental movement patterns of modern skiing, your trust in your ability to react appropriately will be rewarded. It is only necessary to know, but to know very well, functional stance, effective balance, and the fundamental movement patterns, "Wax on, wax off."

INDOOR PRACTICE

The ultimate connection skiers have with their skis is their feet. Other than the need to flex their ankles, many skiers seem oblivious to the role their feet and ankles play in directing the skis. Previously we talked about the innate sense and visual impact of upper body involvement in turning older equipment. Refining our movements to adapt to modern equipment requires increased awareness of the feet, ankles, knees, and thighs; of the entire lower body.

To begin, we will use a few simple analogies to focus your attention. Sign your name on a sheet of paper. To write comfortably, you must maintain enough tension in your fingers to control the pen. Too much tension and the signature becomes jagged and forced (try a signature while squeezing the pen hard). Too little tension and the writing becomes sloppy and uncontrolled (try barely gripping the pen). Similarly, in skiing we require enough tension in our legs and torso to control our descent. Too much and our movements are jerky. Too little and we move sloppily and without a clear direction. Now sign your name again. Notice how most of the writing action is controlled by your fingers and, to a smaller degree, by your wrist and, to a degree smaller still, by your elbow and shoulder. Now sign your name controlling the pen exclusively with the wrist, then the elbow, and finally the shoulder. Each successive signature undoubtedly will be less precise, more cumbersome. The connection to skiing lies in the fact that many skiers rely on large, clumsy movements of the head, shoulders, or torso to turn the skis. Conditions such as heavy, deep snow or the demands of a World Cup giant slalom may require skiers to augment their turning power or ability to balance with these larger, more powerful parts of the body. Skiing under these conditions is analogous to signing your name with a six foot pen. Imagine the movements necessary to accomplish this; the use of the elbows and shoulders would be necessary. Modern skiing requires us to control our equipment from the feet up, as necessary. As we proceed, we will be asking you to sign your name in the snow from your feet up, not from your shoulders down.

Modern ski instructors have found it necessary to change some of the ways they impart information. Because modern movements are so subtle, a demonstration by the instructor doesn't communicate them effectively. It has become necessary to ask students to feel tension in certain muscle groups or to become aware of small pressure differences inside the boot. "Follow me" was the standard, and sometimes the exclusive, teaching approach used in the past. Following a great skier is still of great value. A picture is still worth a thousand words;

however, when the picture no longer has such bold strokes, something more is required. Following a skier provides the big picture of how to perform, but now more than ever skiers require mental patterns and kinesthetic input before they can fully appreciate the subtleties within the big picture.

Balance and Stance

Let's begin our look at stance by examing fore and aft balance and stance. For these exercises you will need only your ski boots, a full-length mirror, and your ski poles or two solid chairs on which you can lean. With your shoes off and standing with your legs fairly straight, focus your weight so that it is over your heels. Move your shoulders quickly from front to back, and monitor how well you are able to maintain your balance over the heels. Experiment with this for one minute. Next, bend your knees and ankles so that your weight is focused over the balls of your feet. Again move your shoulders quickly back and forth and monitor how well you keep your balance. Repeat this for one minute. To reinforce this idea, try doing the same thing on one foot. Spend at least one minute on each leg, first using the heel and then the ball of the foot. Now continue the exercise by focusing your weight over the heel and actually keeping the ball of the foot off the ground, as Doug is doing in Figure 5.1. Rapidly move your shoulders back and forth and monitor your balance. Then focus your weight over the ball of the foot and keep the heel off the ground, as in Figure 5.2. Check your balance. Repeat each exercise a number of times. Many find that it is somewhat easier to balance on the ball of the foot with the added help of the toes. However, they also report a greater amount of muscle strain.

Now try the same exercises with your weight focused over a spot about two thirds of the way back on the arch of the foot, as shown in Figure 5.3. Again, monitor your balance as you move your upper body back and forth. When you can balance comfortably over this spot with both feet on the floor, try standing on only one foot, as Doug is demonstrating in Figure 5.4. Be sure to try this with both the left and the right foot. Most people find it easier to balance on the dominant side. If one side is easier or more comfortable than the other, spend a little more time on the awkward side. Modern skiing requires being able to balance well on either foot.

Figure 5.1

Figure 5.2

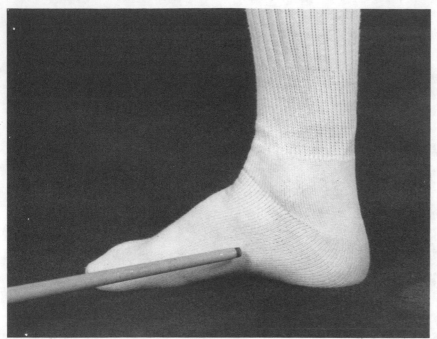

Figure 5.3

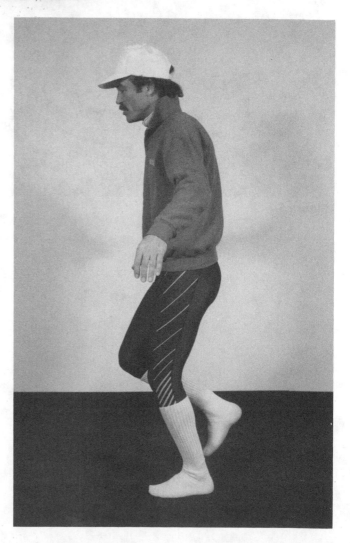

Figure 5.4

As you experiment with balance, you will probably notice that you feel more secure, especially when balancing on one foot, if your foot is allowed to roll to the inside a little. It is natural for the foot to do this when it supports your weight; it is called pronation. Look at Figures 5.5 and 5.6. In Figure 5.5 you can see the arch being elevated, and Doug stands on the outside of his foot. Try this for about thirty seconds. Feel how much muscular force is required. Now let your foot relax, and allow the arch to move closer to the floor, as in Figure 5.6. Notice how much more comfortable and secure you are, and that you are able to balance easily without a lot of strain. In a well-fitted ski boot your foot will not be allowed to roll to the inside; it will be supported under the balance spot so that pressure is transmitted to the ski quickly and accurately. Balancing on the inside of your foot and focusing your weight over the balance spot is critical to modern skiing. To ski effectively, it is important that your foot be supported in this position by your ski boot. Fortunately, modern boots and a skilled boot fitter make this possible for virtually every skier.

Figure 5.5

Figure 5.6

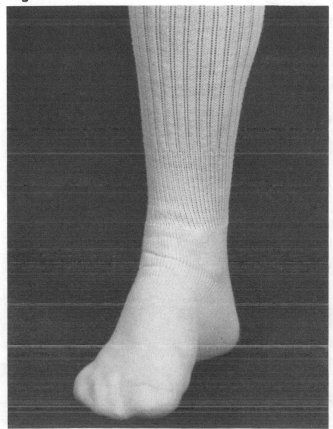

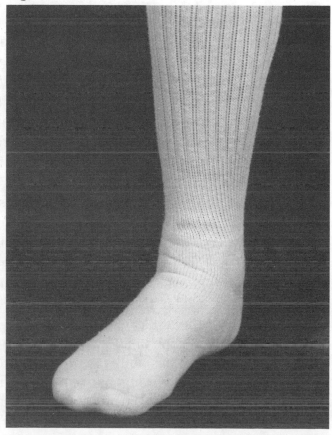

We are spending time on these exercises to illustrate a very important concept: the place from which to balance. Modern, plastic boots were not designed to accommodate skiers who wish to hang forward or lean back. They were designed to allow a quick and positive transfer of instructions from the body to the ski. The body's lack of ability to balance on the ball of the foot or heel should be clearly illustrated by these exercises. This ideal spot over which to balance is less easy to define than the heel or the ball of the foot, since it does not directly come into contact with the floor. Over the last few years we have heard many people (particularly instructors) come up with pet names for this spot such as "the sweet spot," "the button," and even "the B spot" (to give it a little sexual flair). For our purposes, let's refer to it as "the balance spot." This spot then will become the focal point for applying or reducing pressure to the ski. The importance of this point of balance cannot be overemphasized. Any movement in the upper body that prevents us from remaining focused on this point is normally undesirable.

A Functional Range of Motion

With the balance spot in mind, stand with one side of your body toward a full-length mirror. Begin flexing the ankles, knees, and waist in a way that allows you to move up and down and still focus your weight over this spot. You will notice that if you flex too deeply your weight moves over the balls of your feet. Conversely, if you straighten up too far, your weight moves over your heels. Within the flexing and extending that allows you to remain focused over the balance spot is what we can refer to as our "functional range of motion." Continue flexing and extending, looking at your profile on both sides, until your body can move freely and loosely within these limits. As you flex up and down, take note of how each joint flexes. Notice how the ankles, knees, and hips tend to flex equally to achieve this focus of weight over the balance spot. Additionally, feel the muscles that are used in this action, paying particular attention to the muscles of the ankle, calf, and thigh. To go through this inventory may take some time; say, fifteen minutes. Do not rush through it. The motions and muscles we are using in this exercise will be used throughout our skiing. Remember that, although we identified a particular spot in these exercises, it is the ability to move and still remain focused over this spot that helps us achieve our overall goal: balance.

Next, tip your body laterally and support yourself using ski poles or by leaning against a wall or a door jamb. Using the left leg if you are leaning to the right, and vice versa, flex up and down as described earlier. The photo sequence in Figure 5.7 shows Doug performing this exercise. In the first frame he

Figure 5.7

is in a tall stance, as extended as he would ever be in most skiing situations. In the second frame he has a moderately flexed position, and in the third frame he is flexed as deeply as necessary for all but the most extreme situations. The flexing and extending are focused in the outside leg, or Doug's right leg in the pictures. Allow your other leg (the inside one) to passively flex and extend, but do not place much weight on it. Since all turns in skiing require that the body be inside the turning ski, using poles will make these exercises that much closer to actually skiing. Repeat the exercise with the other leg and continue to monitor the muscles used to perform it. Experiment with this for about ten minutes by varying the angle of lean. Now put your ski boots on and perform all the exercises previously mentioned. With boots on, your ability to flex and straighten will be limited. That's fine. Remember that it is your ability to maintain the focus of your weight over the balance spot that is important, not how much you move. It may actually be easier to identify the balance spot with the boot on, since the arch support of most modern boots comes into contact with this spot.

We noted earlier that modern skiers tend to display a taller stance than their predecessors. This difference can be seen in Olympic-caliber skiers and is evident in modern ski instruction. Since modern equipment is so easily encouraged to turn, we seldom need massive flexion and extension movements to disengage the skis from the snow so they can be twisted in the air. This is great news for today's skiers, since each turn no longer requires a major expenditure of energy. This taller stance helps skiers utilize their skeletal structure to deal with the forces present in a turn and to support the majority of their weight. It also allows the musculature to focus on the movements necessary to subtly direct the skis through the turn, and increases the skier's ability to absorb uneven terrain. In short, it is a stronger, more efficient stance.

The Shape of Modern Turns

Before moving on with the movements necessary to make modern, high-quality turns, we will take a look at the shape of these turns. For the vast majority of skiers, the ability to control their speed under a variety of conditions is the ultimate goal.

Figure 5.8

Figure 5.9

Historically, speed control was predominantly a product of skidding through the turn and/or checking. (Checking is the rapid lateral displacement of the skis at the end of the turn. It causes the skis to break away from their original arc and establishes a temporary platform of snow against which to decelerate.) Modern skiers can avail themselves of these actions also. However, it is the shape of the turn and the completion of the arc that should provide most of the speed control for the modern skier.

It has been very common in the past for instructors to draw an S in the snow and bisect it with a vertical line, as shown in Figure 5.8. The accompanying explanation went something like this: As you reach the bisecting line, plant your pole, come up to unweight your skis, twist them into the fall line, and pressure and edge through the arc of the turn. This describes a turn that was valid in the 1970s, and still can be if conditions mandate. The problem for most skiers, however, is that when utilized on packed conditions, this technique creates a great deal of skidding in the start of the turn. When the skis are unweighted, most skiers attempt to quickly twist them into the new direction. Even if the terrain is gentle, past encounters with threatening slopes create an overenergetic response in most skiers. As a result, the skier skids heavily through the first half of the turn and then must attempt to regain control and balance in the last half. The result is a turn whose shape resembles a Z more than an S, as shown in Figure 5.9.

The problem with this Z-shaped turn is that it does not provide effective speed control. Even though the body utilizes this turn shape to minimize speed by spending as little time as possible pointing straight downhill, the shape of this turn lacks the most crucial aspect of speed control: the finish. The idea is not to try to refine this movement. Rather, we will look at movements that encourage the ski to turn in an arc. Merely to minimize this harsh early turning is of little help. The behavior normally recurs as soon as the skier encounters an intimidating situation. Again, the fundamental problem is that normal, thinking human beings do not really trust that their skis want to turn or continue to turn. As mentioned earlier, the difficulty in modern skiing is more mental than physical. It made sense in the past to jump up, twist the body, and whip the skis around. A major reason for the short-ski craze of the early 1970s was that not only were the shorter skis easier to twist, they presented a much less visually intimidating presence than conventional skis. The shorter the ski, the less danger it presented to the skier's psyche. Perceptions are often as important as realities.

Let us now look at a turn with a different shape. In this diagram (Figure 5.10), the focus is on balancing against one ski at a time. You will notice that there is a moment when the weight is on both skis. This merely illustrates that the skier's weight is moving from one ski to the other. You will also notice that the lines become bolder partway through the turn. This signifies an increase in pressure on the ski as it moves through the turn. It is not necessary to make dramatic movements with the body to execute this type of turn. The force of gravity and the skier's own momentum tend to move the weight to the appropriate ski, if this is allowed to happen. In this turn, gravity and momentum help achieve an arc, and it becomes the skier's task to remain balanced and go for a smooth, controlled ride. This occurs in both wedge turns as well as in advanced skiing. In the photo sequence shown in Figure 5.11, Darwyn is demonstrating with his hands the pattern of movement from ski to ski while making a wedge turn. In the first frame, his hands show a turn to his right being finished with the pressure on the left ski (hand). In the second frame, the pressure on the left ski has been released, and in the third frame the right ski has been pressured against the snow. The fourth frame shows the arc of the turn, with the action taking place primarily on the right ski (hand). In Figure 5.12, Darwyn is demonstrating the somewhat quicker pattern of a parallel turn. In the first frame, the turn is being finished on the left ski (hand) while the right ski is being prepared to initiate the new turn. The second frame shows the right ski edged and pressured against the snow, creating the arc, while the left ski is gently guided alongside. Creating these arcs with your hands can be very useful preparation for creating them on the snow with your skis. As we said in Chapter IV, motor programs can be transferred from one part of the body to another, so you can start to change the shape of your turns on skis by designing them with your hands.

Figure 5.10

Figure 5.11

1

2

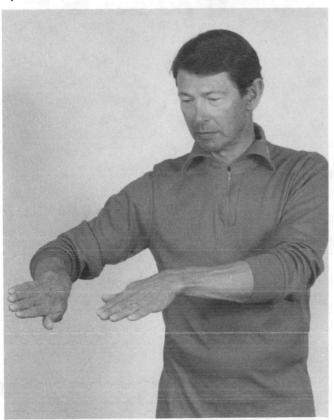

3

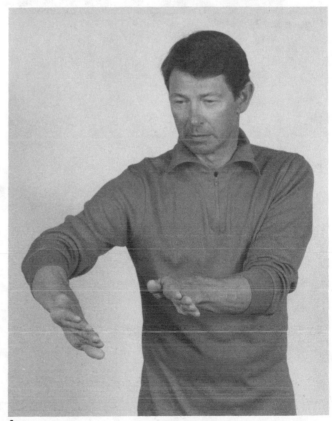

4

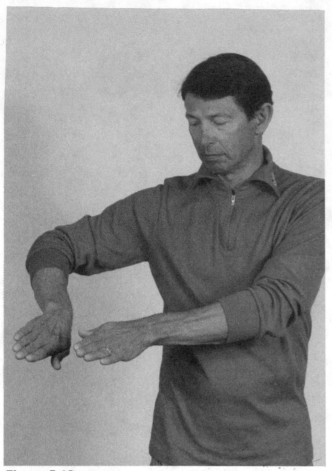 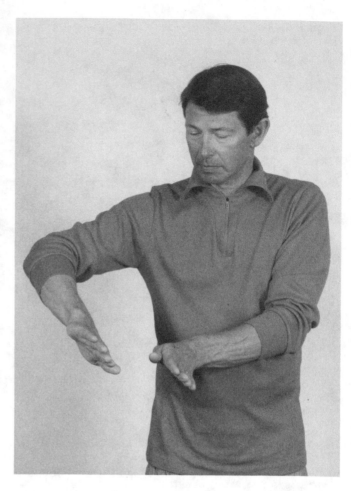

Figure 5.12

Weight Transfer Made Easy

Begin to feel the movements necessary to achieve this turn by taking a short walk around your house. Notice how easily and smoothly your weight is transferred from foot to foot. You will also notice that there is a point at which your weight is on both feet, and then it quickly moves to just one foot. Also sense how the leg flexes slightly and then tenses as it receives your body's weight. Since we have been walking for so long, we are able to achieve this movement with little thought or effort and minimal involvement of the upper body. It is this sense of efficient movement with the focus on the lower body that is the central theme in our approach to modern skiing.

Next try putting your feet fairly close together and hopping along the same path you just walked. Obviously, you can do this, but you must expend a great deal more energy and it is difficult to do it smoothly. This type of movement pattern is much closer to older forms of skiing. This is also the type of movement often displayed by skiers who find themselves in intimidating circumstances.

Consider the movements in a slalom course of any world-class skier over the last ten years. Regardless of nationality or style of the skier, you should be aware that they all move from foot to foot in a way that more closely resembles walking than hopping. We will continue to try and cultivate this type of movement pattern as we move through this chapter. If you felt that the hopping resembled your skiing on the hill, no problem; it just means we have some work to do. If the weight transfer involved in walking felt more like your skiing, great. You are moving in the right direction.

Start the Action in Your Feet

We have spent some time developing awareness in terms of stance as it relates to balance. The importance of lower-body sensitivity cannot be stressed enough. It is a major reason that it is difficult to perceive the subtleties of the movements of modern super-skiers, where so much of the important activity takes place within the boot or within the musculature of the leg. With this in mind, let's try an exercise that demonstrates the difference between the kind of movements we will want to use to begin a turn and the way so many skiers instinctively move.

Begin by sitting down on the edge of a chair, as shown in Figure 5.13. Make sure that your feet are almost directly below your torso. We will be using two different ways of moving starting from this position. First, try standing up and moving slightly forward and to your left at a forty-five degree angle. At first, lead the action with your upper body and shoulders. This will get you up and out of the chair, all right, but you'll probably have to take a step or two to catch your balance, as Doug is doing in the third frame of the sequence. Try this a number of

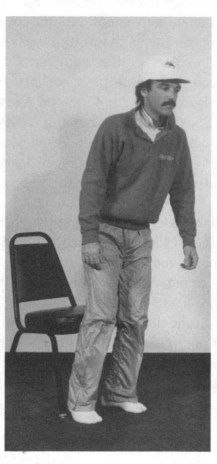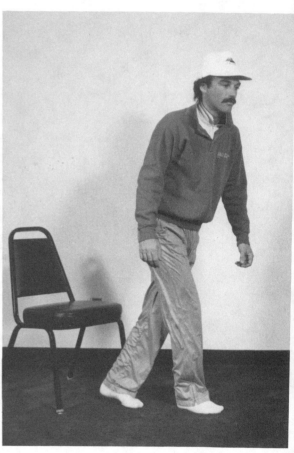

Figure 5.13

times, moving up and to the left, then to the right. Now sit down again and move in the same direction, but this time begin the movement from the feet. In other words, focus the movements so that they begin at and continue to move from the feet. The photo sequence in Figure 5.14 shows Doug doing this, although this is one of the kinds of subtle movements of modern skiing that are hard to see. The first two pictures in the sequence are almost identical to the first two in the last figure. However, you can see the result of initiating this movement in the feet in the

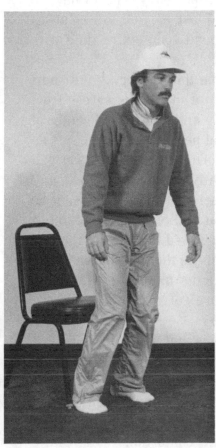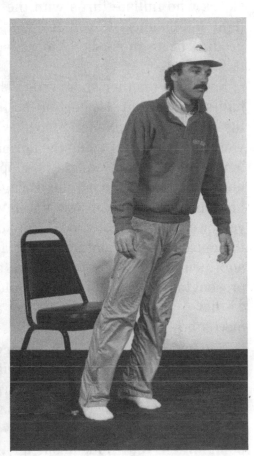

Figure 5.14

third frame; here, Doug is able to find his balance more easily and does not have to take a step. That step would shift weight to the inside ski if he were on skis. Again, move in both directions a number of times. You should feel that the movements that begin in the feet allow you to remain in far better balance than those beginning in the upper body.

The two movements we just explored are two ways of beginning a turn. Imagine the superior sense of balance provided by beginning a turn in the feet rather than the upper body. Skiers initiating turns in their feet tend to remain in balance, while skiers who initiate turns with the upper body tend to have to fight for balance. If you feel that most of your turns are a product of an upper-body focus, spend some extra time with this exercise.

Now take another short walk. This time, though, take short half-steps so that the heel of the front foot lands across from the arch of the back foot. Step slowly and land on the center of your foot instead of using the normal heel-to-toe stride. As you land, feel how your weight is supported by each leg. You will notice again that the leg flexes slightly in the ankle, knee, and hip joint. Be aware of how the muscles of the leg contract as your weight is transferred. First you will feel a contraction in the muscles of the foot and ankle, followed by those in the calf and then along the front and back of the thigh. If no tension is present in the leg, you have just fallen down. Amazingly, though we have walked all our lives, we are seldom aware of these mechanics.

The importance of this knowledge is that with minimal effort we are transferring all of our weight from foot to foot. Look again at the turn diagram in Figure 5.10. All you need to do is straighten out the arcs, and the pattern of weight shift would be about the same in skiing as in walking. This is an important point, when you think about all the contortions skiers have been forced to perform over the years in the name of weight transfer, from picking up one ski and the resultant "kick" to a massive tipping of the upper body over the turning ski. Weight transfer has been treated as a complex problem. With modern equipment, weight transfer can often be accomplished almost as simply as when walking.

Basic Movements for Wedge Turns

Don't even think about skipping this part, especially if you are an advanced skier.

In modern skiing, all of the mechanics necessary for the most advanced skiing are present in the basic wedge turn. There are two reasons advanced skiers allow their skis to remain approximately parallel most of the time. The first is simply fatigue. It is tiring to hold the wedge position for an extended period of time. The second reason has to do with efficiency. When the skis are approximately parallel, the resulting freedom of the legs makes it easier to design the turn shape required for the situation. But there are some important advantages to the wedge position. First, there is built-in speed control, if it is needed. Second, there is a wider base of support, so balance can be more easily recovered. Third, the ski that is to make the turn is already pointed in the correct direction—right ski to the left, and left ski to the right. Finally, the wedge position automatically puts the skis on edge, so that when pressure is applied a turn results. And because all of the mechanical principles are present but not complicated by speed, or the slope's steepness, or a desire to "look good," the wedge is an ideal learning situation. So please don't yield to a self-image that says, "I left the wedge and the stem behind me years ago, and I ain't going back now!" The movements you will learn in the following exercises are truly the basis for modern, efficient skiing. "Wax on, wax off."

Tight leg turns. Assume a small wedge position (toes pointed in, heels out) without shoes. Alternately tighten each leg; the tightness should be similar to the feeling you had when walking with small steps. The tightening, again, should begin in the foot and move to the calf and then to the thigh. The sequence of photos in Figure 5.15 shows Doug in the correct position in all four frames. Darwyn is using a ski pole to point to the parts of the foot and leg where you should feel the muscles tighten. The tightening is sufficient to support your weight, but is not the kind of tension that prevents free movement. It really is similar to subtle adjustments your leg muscles make when you walk. This tightening happens very quickly, the same as when walking. As it happens, you will feel yourself flex the leg you are tightening slightly. As the muscles tense,

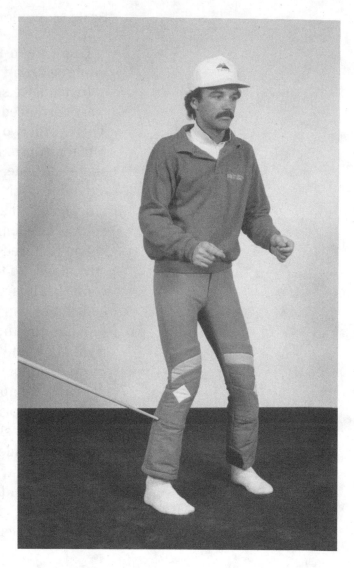

Figure 5.15

they become shorter. Alternate tightening one leg and then the other, as in the differential relaxation technique you learned in Chapter III. In demanding situations on the slope, the tightening will extend all the way up to the abdominal muscles within the stomach. As you do this, you will probably feel a slight rocking from side to side. This is fine, as long as it is a result of actions that originate in the feet. We will be asking you to do this exercise when you reach the slope. Since you will be in the wedge position, the skis will be slightly on edge. As you tighten each leg, you will be putting more pressure on that ski. If the weight change is accomplished by simply tightening your leg, and your wright is focused over the balance spot, the ski will remain on edge and will slice an arc in the snow. If you move using the upper body excessively, or if you pivot your leg, your skis will skid like a car on an icy curve. The feeling of the ski slicing the snow is what we want to achieve. This tightening action, even if done as simply as we have described, will produce the fundamental turn of modern skiing: arcing, not skidding; tail following tip; not smearing.

This action is so important that we want you to repeat this exercise many times. It may seem silly, and in the confines of your living room you might question its validity. But it is a fundamental movement pattern and must be ingrained before encountering the stresses of skiing. "Wax on, wax off." When it feels familiar and can be done quickly and easily, you can begin to use imagery to strengthen this skill so that when you step onto the slope, you are ready to use it in your skiing. Close your eyes and imagine yourself on skis in a slight wedge, gliding slowly forward and down the hill. Focus on the feelings in your feet, as the skis glide over the snow. Be sure that you feel your weight focused over the balance spot. Now, simply tighten your right leg. Feel the right ski begin to slice an arc to the left. Just ride the ski around the arc. As you feel yourself begin to slow down, tighten your left leg and allow the right to relax. Now feel the left ski slice an arc. Again, ride the ski around the arc until it slows and then tighten the right leg, and so forth. Warning: It is not necessary or even healthy to tighten each leg to the point of cramping. Remember the amount of tension used in supporting your weight while walking. Repeat this exercise and the imagery while in your ski boots. Do it many, many times.

Release the old turn to start the new. Now let's take this idea a step further by learning some additional movements we will be using in skiing. Use your ski poles to support yourself laterally by placing them out to the side and slightly forward. (Carpet is highly recommended for this exercise.) Assume a small wedge position, as before. You should feel that the majority of your weight is resting on the inside part of your feet. It seems to help if you do this exercise with your shoes off, but wearing anything short of spike heels will work. Begin the action of moving into a turn (this is similar to the earlier exercise of standing up out of the chair) by first flattening the foot that corresponds to the direction you want to go. If you are moving forward and to the right, begin by flattening the right foot. The photo sequence in Figure 5.16 shows Doug in a

Figure 5.16

balanced stance. In the first frame he is on the inside edges of both skis (feet). The second frame shows his right foot flattened against the floor and his weight supported by his left foot, which is still slightly tipped so that the inside edge of his ski would then be pressured against the snow. To move in this direction, you may try pushing slightly with the other foot, but try instead to push with your arms. The flattening of the foot represents the type of movement we will use to begin turns. We will refer to this as "releasing" the outside ski. To begin a turn, the first thing you must do is to release the downhill ski before encouraging the other to turn. This will become a primary movement for beginning each turn. It is easy to imagine. Picture yourself moving across a slope, in a small wedge, finishing a turn to your left. The majority of your weight will naturally fall on the inside edge of your downhill (right) ski because of gravity. Now feel the pressure on the inside of your right foot, focused over the balance spot. Flatten that foot to release the pressure, and feel your body begin to move to the right as the skis begin their turn down the hill. Rehearse this movement to both sides, varying the intensity of the release. Practice it as shown in Figure 5.16, and then use your imagery skills to begin to experience what it would feel like on the snow.

Once this movement becomes comfortable and you can flatten your foot, releasing the pressure (and the ski), begin to follow the release with an immediate transfer of pressure to the other foot. These movements are almost exactly like the pattern of differential relaxation you learned in Chapter III. Assume a comfortable stance in a slight wedge, balanced against your poles, as shown in Figure 5.17. Tighten your right leg and feel the pressure on the balance spot. Then release that pressure by flattening the foot, and immediately tighten the left leg, as indicated by the arrow in the photograph. On the snow, the release will start the turn and the tightening will continue the turning action. It may be helpful to call out "Release—tighten" as you move from leg to leg. Combine the actions so that they flow smoothly from leg to leg, just as in the differential relaxation exercises. You should also feel a slight flexing and extending as you move. This is fine, since it is a consequence of moving laterally from foot to foot.

When this pattern of movement becomes familiar and easy to accomplish, it is time to use some imagery to begin to transfer the movements to the slopes. Assume the initial wedge

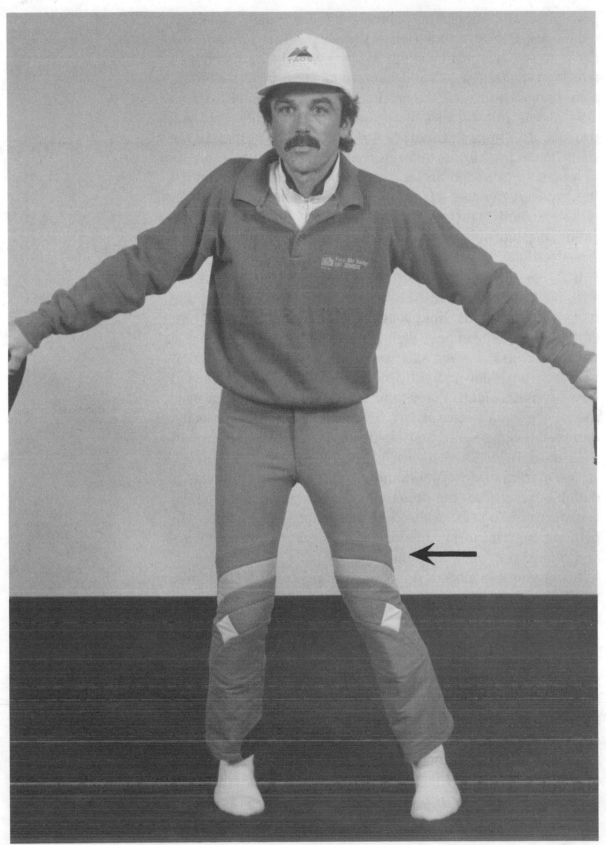

Figure 5.17

position again, supporting yourself on your poles, and close your eyes. Begin to experience yourself gliding forward and down an easy slope, in a small wedge, evenly balanced on both feet. Now tighten your right leg, producing a turn to the left. Ride that turn around the arc until you feel yourself begin to slow down; then release the pressure on your right foot and transfer it to your left foot. Feel the skis begin to turn to the right (down the hill) as you release, and feel the turn continue in a smooth, rounded arc as you tighten the left leg. Maintain the pressure on the left leg until the turn is finished, then release it and transfer it to the right leg. Imagine yourself skiing through a series of smooth, rounded turns with this "release-tighten" pattern of movement.

It is possible to rehearse this pattern with your hands as well. Look again at Figure 5.11, where Darwyn is demonstrating turns with his hands. Hold your hands comfortably out in front of you, in a wedge shape, slightly off to your right. Tip them to the inside, just as your skis would tip. Then flatten your left hand and push down slightly on the right hand as you move it forward and around. When your hands have described a nice, rounded arc and have moved to the left side of your body, flatten the right hand, and push down, forward, and around with the left to make a turn in the other direction. Make a series of turns with your hands, being sure that there is a definite release at the initiation of each turn, followed by transferring the pressure to the other hand. This practice will help you start to form a motor program that you can activate and refine once you are on the snow.

When you are able to draw smooth arcs with your hands, and you can feel the "release-tighten" pattern in your imagery, repeat the sequence with your ski boots on. Be sure to do the entire sequence of exercises. Be aware of the balance spot as the place from which pressure is released and the place to which pressure is transferred after releasing it from the other foot. Monitor your movements in a full-length mirror to be sure that you are initiating the release-tighten sequence in your feet and legs. There should be very little movement above the hips, and what there is should only be the result of the release-tighten sequence, not the cause of it.

Refining your turns. Next, sit down on the corner of a chair and place one leg slightly behind you, as Doug is doing in the first frame of Figure 5.18. Place your hand on the corresponding hip and hold it in place as you drag your foot forward, drawing an arc on the floor, as shown in the second and third frames.

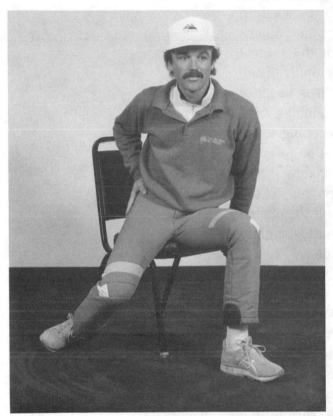 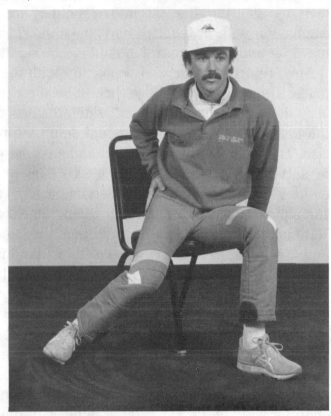

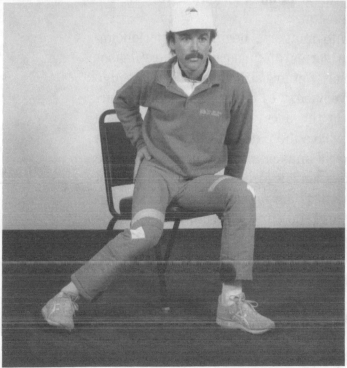

Figure 5.18

Drag the foot against the carpet at least fifteen times for each leg. Notice the muscles that come into play to create this action. You should feel a mild burning in the leg after fifteen repetitions if you are using sufficient pressure. This movement represents the muscular action we will use to shorten the radius of the turn by steering the ski into a tighter arc. It is used in connection with a weighted and edged ski. This action allows the skier additional control in guiding the ski through the turn.

Now, return to your wedge position with the support of the poles. Tighten your right leg, just as in the exercises we have been doing, except that as you tighten the new outside leg, add the muscular action you felt while doing the preceding exercise. This combination of tension and steering will be referred to as engaging the new turning ski. (You won't actually be making the leg arc in this exercise. Just make sure you feel the same muscles come into play as when you were on the chair.) You may notice that with this addition, the leg rotates slightly and the knee seems to move slightly to the inside. A little of this is fine, but the knee should move only slightly and the hip should move hardly at all. Neither the hip nor the torso are twisted into the turn. This is another one of those subtle muscular actions that are so critical in modern skiing. Now practice the movements, shifting the action from leg to leg. You may find it helpful to say out loud, "Release—engage; release—engage." Remember, engaging is a combination of tension and steering activity. Practice this a number of times, varying the intensity of steering and tension.

To carry this pattern into imagery, begin by experiencing yourself making a smooth series of turns using the release-tighten sequence. Remember, you are still using a small wedge position, so the turns are very easy to initiate and to complete. Pay attention to the size of the arcs you are making in this pattern of turns. When you have the pattern well established in your imagery, begin to add the muscular tension you felt in the chair exercise. Adding this steering force will make the arc of the turn shorter. The ski will come around more quickly, but still in a smooth, rounded arc. You can help yourself learn this pattern by saying "Release—engage" as you move from turn to turn. Now try to vary the amount of steering force you apply. More steering produces quicker turns; less steering produces longer-radius turns. In your imagery, establish a pattern of turns of a particular size, and then deliberately change the pattern by changing the amount of steering force. Be sure that you are focused on lower body movements. Your image should be of a smooth flow of forces generated in the feet and legs, with your upper body quietly balanced, just along for the ride.

From the Wedge to the Basic Parallel Turn

There is no "trick" to parallel skiing. As we have said, all the basic mechanical components of modern skiing are used in the wedge turn. You don't have to do anything extra to ski with your skis pointed in approximately the same direction most of the time. When you are skilled at the basic components of balance, lateral movement, and engaging the new outside ski, the inside ski naturally aligns with the outside ski. Even advanced parallel skiers can benefit from turning their attention to fundamentals. If you try to force the skis into a parallel position before it is ready to happen, you are quite likely to resort to gimmicks, like "the kick." If you turned immediately to this section to find out how to "ski parallel," go back to page one—there is no magic potion here. If, on the other hand, you have worked your way patiently through this book, you have by now built or refined the skills that will allow you to balance efficiently against the inside edge of the outside ski. The beauty and grace of modern skiing is in the use of the controlling ski; most of the time the other ski just assumes a ready position, which happens to be approximately parallel. If that hasn't happened for you yet, keep developing your ability to balance against the outside ski, and it will. Patience.

The following exercises are simply a continuation of the skills you have already developed. We will use the "release-engage" sequence, just as in the wedge turns, but we will allow the muscles in the thighs and pelvis to assume a more relaxed position. Using your poles for support, allow your feet to be parallel but still comfortably apart. Now you will be moving laterally with very little forward movement. To begin, tip to your left by releasing any pressure from the left foot and engaging the right foot. You should wind up in approximately the position in which you see Doug in the first frame of Figure 5.19. Now release your right foot and allow your left arm to move you laterally over your feet, as in the second frame of the sequence. Then tip to the other side, engaging the left leg and supporting your weight on your right arm. Within the confines

Figure 5.19

of a living room, we must approximate the forces present in skiing. When moving across the slope and through a turn, forces build that seek to throw the skier to the outside of the turn. By maintaining tension in our outside leg and tipping that leg enough to keep the ski on its inside edge, we are able to resist this impulse. In this simulation, we are using the arms to approximate the effects of these forces on the body.

To accomplish this lateral movement while skiing, we usually need only to release the turning ski and allow the forces to move our bodies in the direction of the new turn. The first frame of Figure 5.20 shows Doug resisting the pull of a bungee cord. This represents the forces encountered in the last half of the turn. In the second frame, Doug has released his left foot and allowed the force to move him laterally. At this point, he is in a good position to engage the right foot and begin the new turn. While skiing, this release not only helps put us in a position to engage the new turning ski, but actually begins the turn, if we allow the body to move in the direction of the new turn. This is a prime example of working with the forces present in skiing rather than fighting against them.

Practice and review this movement many times. Try varying the width of the poles to approximate different amounts of force in the turn. Also vary the tempo to approximate turns of different sizes.

This release-engage pattern, which allows the body to move in the direction of the new turn, is the basis for all modern skiing. We know it seems simple. It *is* simple, at least in concept. It becomes more difficult as the distractions of speed, steepness, obstacles, and other skiers are encountered on the slopes. It is especially difficult if you have another picture in your mind; say, a vision of the classic skier. So it is critically important to do as much work as possible to establish this movement pattern before you encounter those distractions, and imagery is one of the best ways to accomplish this.

For your first imagery sessions with this movement pattern, take your shoes off, get your ski poles, and assume a balanced position on both feet. Place the poles on the carpet so that you have enough room to move laterally but not so much that you have to work hard to support your weight. Now close your eyes, and let your weight fall onto the right pole while you engage with the left leg. Experience yourself moving to your right, in a shallow traverse across a moderate slope. Feel the pressure

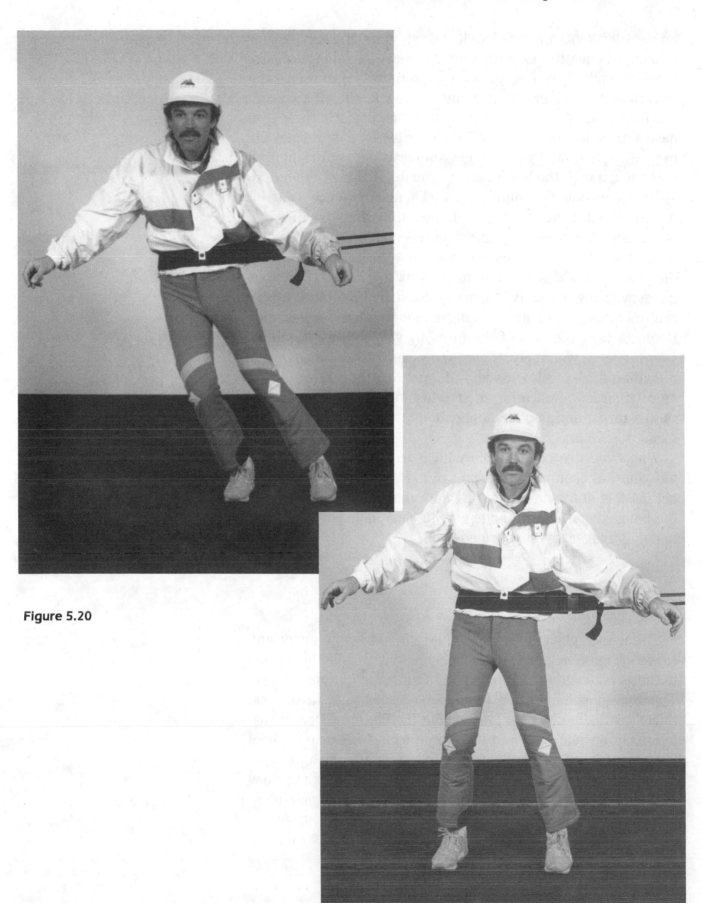

Figure 5.20

on your left foot, then release it. As you move laterally to your left, experience the skis (in your imagery) beginning to move down the hill. Now engage with your right foot and leg, and experience your right ski turning to the left, slicing a smooth arc in the snow. Ride the ski around the arc, and when you have started to slow down, release the right foot, move laterally to your right so that you are now supported on your right arm, and engage with the left foot. Now you are turning to the right, again in a smooth, rounded arc. Then experience yourself moving from turn to turn with just this simple pattern of movement: "Release—engage; release—engage."

After you have done this exercise a few times, begin to notice the size and shape of the turns you are making in your imagery. They probably are pretty consistent in size, and you probably have been maintaining about the same speed, too. Begin to vary the size of the turns by varying the amount of steering force you apply. If necessary, refresh your memory by repeating the exercise shown in Figure 5.19 (pp. 110–11). Use a more vigorous application of steering force to create shorter-radius turns, and gentler applications to create longer-radius turns.

When you are comfortable with this pattern of movement, put your ski boots on and start again. First do the exercise, to get the feel of the movement. Be sure that the pressure is over the balance spot as you engage with each foot. Then move on to doing imagery with your boots on.

Pole Plants with a Purpose

The use of poles in modern skiing is extremely important. However, improper use is very common and it could be argued that it is better to use no pole plant than an inappropriate one. The role of poling action has changed somewhat in the last thirty years. Today, poling is seldom the platform from which to launch unweighting and therefore turning. In some kinds of skiing, such as giant slalom racing, pole plants have even ceased to be used, since they tend to break the skier's flow from turn to turn, and thus their speed. The double pole plant has even made a bit of a comeback, since it helps keep racers aligned with their skis. A single pole plant is normally sufficient, however, and this is the one we will be using.

To begin, let's deal with some terminology. The term "pole plant" seems to indicate that the pole is shoved into the snow, fertilized, and left to sprout. A more appropriate term might be "pole touch," indicating that the pole merely flicks the snow. In any case, the terms will be used interchangeably. A certain amount of impact to the body is present as turns become shorter. In extremely quick turns, the pole can be used to stop the upper body momentarily, allowing the lower body to turn beneath it. Mogul skiing and heavy powder conditions are also situations in which pole action affects the upper body to a greater degree. However, a general rule for pole action is that only minimal weight is placed on the pole.

The timing of the pole plant is of great concern. In the past, pole plants usually marked the movement or initiation of the new turn. This timing is still used in modern skiing, particularly if some braking action is desired or if the turn seems difficult to initiate. If continued speed and acceleration are desired, the pole touch often occurs after the initiation of the new turn.

Two important aspects of pole action that can be developed at home are timing and the positioning of the hands for effective pole use. One of the most frustrating situations an instructor or coach faces is when they must teach or correct pole action. During this process, the skier often loses touch with the movements in their legs that effectively turn their skis. This is inevitable, since we humans are not always able to concentrate fully on two subjects at once. Practicing pole action at home can be of great value on the slope if, through the practice, the action of pole preparation, touching, and hand positioning are ingrained.

Begin by grabbing your poles and proceeding to the largest carpeted area you can find. Lawns or beach areas work fine if they are available. Tightly grip the handles of both poles and then relax the bottom two fingers of both hands. With your hands held comfortably in front of you, swing one pole forward with the wrist, and touch the floor slightly ahead of you. The relaxed bottom two fingers should allow the tip of the pole to swing freely. Keeping the hand in the same spot, bring the pole's tip back behind your feet. Do the same thing with your other pole. Try this a number of times with each hand. Next, touch one pole and then, as soon as you begin to bring it back, begin to swing the other forward to make the touch. Try to keep the action going, so that one touch leads directly to the next. Vary the tempo of the swing. Practice this often, possibly while carrying on a conversation or watching TV. It is important that you become able to perform this action without having to concentrate on it. Remember, the hands should remain comfortably in front of you and relatively stationary.

Figure 5.21

Next, try walking in an S-shaped pattern similar to the round turns you will make on the slope. Swing the pole as before and touch it as you begin to start the next arc. In Figure 5.21, you can see Doug walking to his left in the first frame and touching the pole to the ground to initiate the turn back to his right. In the second frame, he is in the middle of the turn.

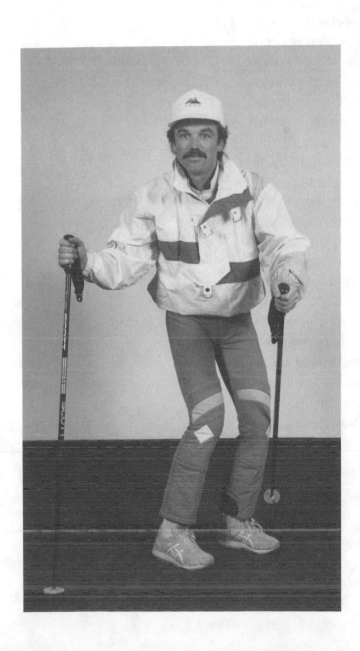

Notice that he has kept both hands in a relaxed but ready position. In the third frame he is completing the turn to his right and is touching the left pole to the ground to initiate the next turn. Note: You should feel some of the same sensation when you release your foot to start the new arc and the same tension in the leg as in the previous exercises. In the long arcs, allow your upper body to follow along in the direction you are moving. In the short arcs, keep the upper body facing straight ahead as the legs change direction. In both cases, try to time the swing of the pole so that the touch starts the new arc. If you are unsure about which pole to use, think of the right pole as starting the arc to the right and the left pole as starting the arc to the left.

Imagery is not especially helpful in developing effective pole action. There are just too many ways errors can creep in, and then you would be practicing mistakes instead of effective movements. We would rather have you use your imagery sessions to build the fundamental movement patterns of the lower body. In addition, there are a number of drills you can do to establish good habits for pole use. Try running through the arcs on a lawn or beach, using the pole touch to initiate each new arc. The forces present in this exercise can help approximate the forces you will encounter while skiing. For those interested in racing and acceleration, try running through long arcs in which the pole touch is just after the start of the change of direction. You may feel a little funny running around planting your poles in your neighborhood park, but you will be glad you did when you reach the slope.

At this point you may be wondering, "Is that all there is?" Well, no. But these exercises will help you learn the fundamental movement patterns of modern skiing, and mastering them will enable you to find out how much there *really* is to skiing. Developing a high level of proficiency in applying these skills while on the snow will allow you to explore the steeps, the bumps, the powder, the race course, *toute neige, toute montagne.*

Mountain Application 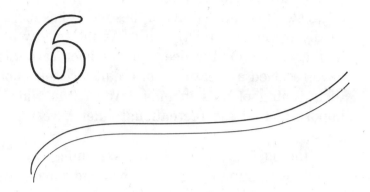 6

GETTING THE SEASON OFF TO A GREAT START

Preparation can certainly help you get the most out of your ski season. In physical preparation, the skier should try for a balance between flexibility and strength. Even though downhill skiing tends to be an anaerobic sport, a blend of aerobic and anaerobic training is ideal. This helps endurance (especially at high altitudes) and the ability to be explosive in higher-level skiing situations. Modern fitness instructors should be able to provide a good program for achieving these goals. If you are unable to achieve "total fitness" before your ski trip, mild stretching immediately prior to the trip, and movement such as a brisk walk immediately prior to your first run, is useful in the short run. This warming up and limbering of the muscles in connection with progressive muscle relaxation presented in Chapter III can be helpful in preventing injuries and in performing well. Preseason honing of your imagery skills will also pay big dividends in better skiing and more fun.

The Importance of Ski Tuning

You have heard us refer to the ski as a tool. We have also suggested that the quality of these tools has increased geometrically in the last thirty years. As the quality of the tool has increased, so has the need for precision care. Ski technicians have received a great deal of credit for their choice of wax or their tuning of skis in many World Cup wins. It is equally important that the recreational skier have well-tuned equipment.

In the past, the goal of most ski tuning was to help the ski "hold" by making the edges sharp and square. Because of the advent of modern construction techniques and materials, today's skis require a different approach to tuning. Modern skis are much more responsive than older models, and it is possible for a ski to be too sharp and to hold too well. Proper tuning enhances the performance of modern skis, but improper tuning can make them completely unmanageable.

Basically, skis flex in two different planes. One is longitudinal, which refers to the flex along the ski's length. The other is torsional, which refers to the ski's resistance to twisting. Skis designed for racers thirty years ago were very stiff in both planes to deal with the speed as well as the forces the racer experienced. It was a difficult ski to handle; however, it did provide the needed stability. For the less accomplished skier, skis were slightly softer, but were still quite stiff and unruly, since they had to have enough integrity to hold a turn. One of the greatest developments of modern ski engineering is to have differentiated these planes of flexion. Designers have created skis that can flex softly lengthwise yet remain firm enough torsionally to provide control, even on hard surfaces. These developments have provided wonderful options for skiers at all levels. However, these easy-turning, solid-holding darlings can turn into monsters if they have not been carefully prepared.

To shed more light on this specialized skill, we asked Dana and Danny Brienza of Looney Tunes in Taos Ski Valley, New Mexico, to talk about a differentiated approach to tuning modern skis. They have owned and operated a successful custom tuning shop for fifteen years, and have helped many recreational and professional skiers enjoy the sport.

Tuning modern skis. The Brienzas told us the following:

"Ski tuning, as with ski technique, has gone through an evolution these past decades. As skis changed from wooden boards to synthetic laminates, so did the methods used to keep them smooth and sharp. Today's skis can be manufactured to flex easily in one direction—for instance, longitudinally—yet remain very stiff torsionally. Skis have thereby become more responsive and more precise, not to mention more fun. Another result is that proper ski tuning has never been more important.

Skiers as far back as the late 1800s have shown enthusiasm for the care of their equipment. They made home-brewed potions for waxing their skis, using wood oils and beeswax to keep their skis gliding across the snow. They called it "doping" their skis, and many ski-dope ingredients were top secret. The methods for maintaining skis have changed, but the enthusiasm remains. Skiers today are becoming more aware that ski tuning isn't for experts only. Every skier benefits from well-tuned equipment. Beginners can progress more quickly if they can count on their skis to turn easily and hold when they use their edges. A good tune-up adds predictability and can even help make skiing a safer sport. The predictable edge is equally valuable to the expert skiing the steeps, or the racer on the course testing his limits. The care you put into your equipment will be paid back to you in pure skiing pleasure.

"Some of the repairs your skis might need will be obvious. It's easy to see holes and scratches in the plastic base material. These areas catch snow and cause friction in the turn, and thus you'll have to put more effort into your skiing. When these areas are filled with plastic and smoothed, the skis will glide more easily, for smoother, more efficient turns. If these repairs are neglected for too long, you could damage your skis beyond repair.

"It is often more difficult to see problems with the edges than it is to see scratches in the base. Perhaps the most significant step in ski tuning is the work done on the edges. When they are sharp, smooth, and free of burrs, the skier will enjoy the best response. The shape of the ski from edge to edge also affects performance. Even the advent of groomed ski trails and hard-packed snow surfaces makes precision ski tuning a necessity. If your edges are even slightly "railed," it can feel like you're riding an unbroken bronco. On a railed ski, both edges are higher than the base material, and when turned bottom up, the ski resembles a railroad track. Because it is a matter of a few millimeters, railing is hard to see without using a machinist's straight edge, but it is easy to feel when initiating a turn. A railed ski doesn't slide from side to side or carve easily. It may hook suddenly or track straight. It's difficult to make smooth, subtle turns when your skis are like this, because your edges hang down and grab the snow. You'll find yourself forcing the skis to skid sideways, using lots of valuable energy to do so. Even brand-new skis need to be properly finished before their first test drive. This finish cannot be achieved by one run over the belt grinder. Grinders are effective for sharpening the metal edge, but shaping the ski is accomplished best by hand-filing. Remember that a ski tune is not a standardized product. Each ski shop may sell completely different services with their ski tune. We don't believe a tune-up is complete without checking the shape of the ski base with a hand file. The way the skis are finally shaped can be personalized to fit the skier and the equipment. Skiers at all ability levels deserve a tune-up that is correct for the way they ski. That skier can put more power into skiing because skis with properly shaped edges, free of burrs and honed to a silky sharpness, result in a smooth, efficient turn. The skier can easily roll onto their edge and then get off that edge between turns. When it's time to run 'em straight, you'll be gliding on the plastic base; ready to go to the edge when you need to. Finally, the metal edge on the tips and tails, where the skis curve up off the snow past the running surfaces, should be dulled.

"Waxing is the last, loving step of a great tune-up. Wax does more than make your skis go fast. Wax helps your skis glide from side to side for easy turning. It also acts as a conditioner and protector for the plastic base. There is also something about the ritual of hot-waxing your skis carefully with your own "potion" that makes you feel good about your equipment. Take good care of your skis and they will take good care of you!"

The Importance of Ski Boots that Fit

To precisely control our turning tools (or skis), we need a boot that is matched and fitted properly to our individual feet. It is not always easy to find a good boot fitter; however, the search is well worth the trouble. Here in Taos, we are blessed with a number of fine boot technicians. We asked Bob Gleason to help you gain a greater understanding of the important aspects of boot fitting. Gleason is a highly regarded "boot guru" whose insights appear in many national publications.

The art and science of boot fitting. Bob Gleason says, "Balance is defined as standing efficiently through the use of the individual's anatomical structure. When an individual is in their optimal skeletal alignment, muscles can be used efficiently to perform the dynamic movements of skiing. If skeletal alignment is not optimal, muscles that could be effective in driving skis are instead used to stabilize the skier.

"The foot is a complex mechanical device. Fifty-six bones are wrapped in a pair of plastic ski boots. That is more than a quarter of the bones in the human body. The foot is amazing; consider that in running, it absorbs the shock of around twelve times the person's weight, then serves as a lever that propels the runner onward. Skiing is something the foot was never designed to do. So, to compensate for this, we have developed supportive plastic ski boots and orthotic footbeds. If the boots and orthotics are doing their job properly, the skis become an extension of the skier's skeletal structure. If the boots and orthotics are not performing, the skier's capabilities are impaired.

"In walking and running, a major role of the foot is to function as a shock absorber. Thus, most people's arches drop when they apply weight to the foot. This flattening of the foot allows the bones of the feet to spread, in the shock-absorbing motion known as pronation. If a person had an ideal foot, as the step progressed from heel-strike toward toe-off, the arch would rise back up and out of pronation; thus, instead of the bones of the feet remaining spread apart and acting as a shock absorber, they would realign, forming a firm lever ready to propel the walker forward.

"Since most of mankind evolved stumbling through rough, broken terrain, shock absorption, in the form of pronation, took precedence over leverage. Most of us have feet which remain pronated through our stride. When a foot remains pronated in a ski boot, the skier uses the muscles of the foot for balance rather than standing with a firm skeletal structure. To be supple and at the same time powerful in skiing, the muscles of the foot and ankle need to be available to pressure and steer the ski. A well-constructed orthotic footbed supports the foot in a more stable posture. Mainly by cupping the heel bone, and secondarily by supporting the arch and matching the contours of the front part of the foot, an orthotic reduces excess pronation. So a well-constructed orthotic enhances a skier's ability to stand over the bone structure of the foot, improving balance and power.

"The boot should mate to the foot exactly. It should create firm, smooth containment of every portion of the foot that the boot encapsulates. If a foot pronates, it spreads in the boot every time the skier weights the foot. When the foot is unweighted, it contracts as the arch rises. This motion can cause severe abrasion of the skier's foot. In order to have a smoothly contained boot fit, the bottom of the foot must rest on a firm foundation. The most effective way to create that foundation is with an orthotic footbed.

"Most people buy boots that are a little too big. The materials in the inner boot compress with use. Skiing creates tremendous forces that quickly reduce the resiliency of foams, nylons, and fabrics in the inner boot. So, with use, ski boots become larger. It is important to the control of a pair of skis that there be no excess motion between the foot and the ski boot. So the new boot should fit very tightly—almost uncomfortably tight. A new ski boot should feel like a very firm handshake. It should wrap the foot snugly on every side. A new boot should not require buckling or the closing of the boot's tightening mechanisms much beyond their loosest settings.

"It is good that a number of manufacturers produce ski boots. Different designers have different concepts as to how their boots should fit. Some boots are narrower; others are wider. Some are thin around the ankle, others bulge out. A good boot fitter will direct the skier to a boot that mates as well as possible to that skier's foot. From there, padding, shell stretching, and liner alterations can fine-tune the boot, creating a consistent match between anatomy and casing.

"Canting allows the adapting of the shape of the boot to the shape of the skier's legs. An individual should not be knock-kneed or bowlegged when skiing. Anything other than a straight-line relationship of the bones of the leg puts undue stress on the knees, requires excessive muscle use to apply pressure to the ski's edge, and has a negative impact on balance. Canting, through boot cuff or sole adjustments, allows the boot to be adapted so that the bones of the leg can form a straight line when the boot's sole is flat. In skiing, a correctly canted boot allows subtle yet powerful control of the ski's edge.

"Discomfort in a ski boot can be the result of several things: a misalignment of the foot, a misalignment of the boot shaft, a bad match between the shape of the boot and the shape of the foot, poor boot design, boot deterioration to the point that the inner boot materials do not have the resiliency needed to cushion the leg and foot, or degradation of the boot shell so it no longer flexes or controls the ski. Misalignment of the foot is dealt with through orthotic footbeds. Misalignment of the boot shaft is controlled through cant adjustment or padding. Mismatch between foot and boot is eliminated through padding, stretching the boot shell, altering the inner boot, or by changing to a boot that better matches the shape of the foot. Other causes of discomfort can sometimes be eliminated through performing alterations on a boot, such as riveting the boot, altering the plastic through cutting or adding material, or changing the hardware. Other situations require replacement of the boot.

"A skier's best friend is a competent boot fitter. Find one, pay what the fitter is worth, and make sure your fitter gets ski time."

The importance of bindings. Modern release bindings have done more than any other innovation to help make skiing a safer sport. This should be the last place to try and save money, yet often skiers recycle bindings on successive sets of skis. *Every* year, have a manufacturer's certified binding mechanic lubricate and test your bindings. Spring fatigue and worn antifriction components are not always obvious. No one cares more about your safety than binding manufacturers and binding technicians. If they tell you it is time to replace your bindings, please listen to them.

APPLYING YOUR INDOOR PRACTICE ON THE SNOW

The preparation is over, and it is finally time to ski. The following exercises are presented to "tune the skier in" to modern skiing. Our hope is that you will go through the following progression of movements during the first few days of each ski season. A quick review while taking a run or two could also be helpful, if you mysteriously lose your focus in midseason or if it has been long since your last trip. After initial practice, follow your desires, be they free skiing, a race clinic for Nastar, bumps, or a private lesson in powder skiing. Take these movements, use them, and then go and have a ball.

Stance. Begin by proceeding immediately to an easy, groomed run. Once off the lift, take a moment to find the balance spot. Experiment with tipping your weight forward on the balls of the feet and toes and then back on heels. Tip back and forth until you are certain you have identified your balance spot. From there, flex up and down, continuing to maintain your focus on the balance spot. This process should take just a few minutes.

Excessively forward

Excessively back

Magic turns. Now, move onto the slope and assume a comfortable wedge position facing down the hill. We are now going to make our first direction changes, called magic turns. All you need to do to make these happen is to start down the hill, look in the direction you want to go, and *believe* that your skis will take you there. Continue to look and believe, and allow the turn to continue. The turn will proceed slowly; before the skis slow down dramatically, look in the other direction and allow the skis to turn that way. As your momentum builds, the turns should occur even more easily.

The magic is in the discovery of how little energy is required to encourage modern equipment to turn. It is not necessary to

Magic turn start

twist your head or shoulders. In fact, if your turns do not seem to be working, chances are that you are doing far too much to make them happen. Merely allow the body to move with the turn. You should notice that your weight naturally shifts to the outside ski as you turn. Try a series of eight to ten of these turns two or three times. We find this exercise particularly effective with advanced skiers. This group's first run of the year is often marked by a series of "linked recoveries" in an effort to warm up. No matter what your level, give it a try. It only takes a few minutes and can often provide some interesting insights. After all, it is magic!

Magic turn mid-point

Wedge-tighten. Now face across the hill and take a few short steps. Monitor how your musculature contracts to support your weight: first the foot, then the calf, followed by the upper leg. Make a series of wedge turns similar to the magic turns. Add the tightening of the outside leg to begin and to continue each turn as shown on pages 132–33. It may help to think to yourself,

Tightening left leg

"Tighten; tighten." The additional weighting of the outside leg will provide a quicker, more positive turn than previously. Make sure not to move the hips over the turning ski. Allow the pressure to build against the inside edge merely through tightening the leg. Try this series of turns a number of times, varying the amount of tension and the size of the turn.

Tightening right leg

Wedge turn with right leg

Release-tighten. To begin, face across the hill standing in a small wedge. Flatten the downhill ski and allow the body to move down the hill. You will notice that the flattened ski will immediately start to move and turn downhill. This is the release action we spoke of in Chapter V. Try this a number of times on each leg so that each time you flatten your downhill foot the ski begins to move. Begin another series of wedge turns. This time, angle slightly across the hill with the downhill leg tight-

Tight left leg

ened. To begin the first turn, release the tightened leg by flattening the foot and allowing the body to move in the direction of the new turn. As soon as you feel the turn begin, tighten the other leg and ride the arc. Try three or four series of these turns while thinking, "Release—tighten." Experiment with the amount of tension and intensity of the release to create different-sized turns.

Left leg release

Release left leg

Tight right leg

Release-engage. Move to slightly steeper, groomed terrain. Find a relatively flat spot and take your skis off. Support yourself laterally with your poles. Drag one leg at a time to form an arc in the snow. Repeat this action about fifteen times for each leg, or until there is a mild tingling in the muscles you are using. Put your skis back on and try another series of turns. This time add this steering action to the leg that is tightened. This combination of tightening and steering becomes "engage." Reduce the amount of wedge slightly, and proceed across the hill. Release the downhill leg and allow the body to move with the turn. Engage the new turning leg and continue to tighten and steer (engage) through the turn as illustrated on pages 140–41. Use the idea of "release—engage" to make a series of turns.

Left leg engage

Release left leg

Continue to use "release—engage," and gradually make the wedge smaller and allow a small increase in speed. At this point, because of the forces present in the turn, the inside ski will naturally want to align itself with the outside ski through the end of the turn. At that point, it would become uncomfortable for the inside ski to be held in a wedge. Using this natural tendency, gently guide the inside foot parallel through the end of the turn as illustrated on page 143. Caution: This does not

Engage right leg

mean you are bringing the legs and feet close together. You are merely controlling the path of the inside ski so that it corresponds with that of the outside ski. After you finish the turn with your skis parallel, return to the wedge to begin the next turn. Practice these turns a number of times. Now add the pole touch to these turns. Touch the downhill pole just prior to the release of the weighted ski. The pole touch is the signal for the release-engage, now "touch-release-engage." Remember to prepare (swing) the other pole as soon as the first one is touched.

Continue by skiing a number of full runs using these mechanics. Gradually, use a smaller wedge to begin each turn. Also, as you become more comfortable with the movements begin to align the inside foot earlier and earlier in each turn. Experiment with this pattern until the movements flow and connect.

Basic parallel turns. Beginning in a comfortable parallel stance, angle slightly across the hill and allow some speed to build. Touch the pole, release the downhill ski, and engage the new outside ski. Continue to guide the outside ski through the arc while preparing the pole for the upcoming turn. The mechanics here are exactly the same as in the last section, except that you are no longer starting from a wedge position. You may also find that it helps increase the intensity of the release of the weighted ski to put the body in a position such that the engagement of the new outside ski occurs on its inside edge. A slight increase in speed and slightly steeper terrain will also encourage the parallel turn.

This is the basic turn of modern skiing. You may want to ski these turns for the entire afternoon of your first day on the slopes. Try varying the size of your turns from short to long, and experiment with different amounts of release and engage. Also vary the type of terrain on which you practice these movements. Keep in mind that speed control is determined by the degree to which the turn is finished. If on slightly steeper terrain, continue to guide the outside ski for a longer period of time.

If you find that you are still wedging at the beginning of each turn, seek flatter terrain and make turns that do not come so far across the hill. Another possibility is that you have not yet really become proficient in the release-engage sequence. Remember that it requires you to be balanced against the "balance spot," able to transfer your weight smoothly to the new outside ski while releasing the old ski, and able to guide the ski through the turn with appropriate steering force. Also, remember what we told you in Chapter V: There is no gimmick to parallel skiing. Sound fundamentals will produce a parallel skier; tricks won't work. So, spend some more time with the wedge turn sequence we have been building here and in Chapter V. As these turns become more comfortable try changing your mechanics so that the pole touch occurs after the release of the new inside ski. This will help add to the flow and rhythm of your turns. Finally, if you feel that you have hit a plateau and can't find the way off it, have a lesson with a qualified instructor. He or she will be able to see which of the skills is lacking, or not well enough developed, and to suggest solutions.

Tuning in to Modern Turning

Photocopy or tear out this page and keep it in your pocket while you ski. It is a guide to the fundamentals you have been learning.

ACTION	EXERCISE FOCUS	TERRAIN	TIME
Stance	Balance Spot	Flat	5 min.
Magic Turns	Believe	Beginner	5 min./series of 3
Wedge-Tighten	Small Steps	Beginner	10 min./series of 3
Release-Tighten	Release	Easy/ Intermediate	10 min./series of 3
Release-Engage	Steering	Intermediate	1 hr./3 runs
Basic Parallel	Increase Release	Intermediate	3 hr./5 runs

ADVANCED MOVEMENTS

The movements and actions presented in the previous exercises should benefit skiers at virtually any level. In an effort to "keep it simple," we have resisted including a vast number of special interests. The personal attention of a qualified instructor or coach can be extremely helpful in focusing and refining your interests. Specialty books can also be valuable, once the fundamentals are in place. However, to get some perspective on how these basics might be applied, and some special applications, we present the following.

Long-radius, high-speed turns. At high speeds the skier must deal with increased external forces in each turn. To balance against these forces, it is necessary to tip to the inside of the turn. This can best be accomplished by tipping the turning leg progressively as these forces build. The inside leg moves uphill and out of the way to allow the weighted leg room to adjust and balance as needed.

Short-radius turns. Increased steering and/or twisting of the leg or legs can help reduce the arc. As the turns become shorter, the skis tend to pivot under the feet to a greater degree. The body remains facing down the hill. The skis move under the body and are released to the side. This creates a somewhat twisted relationship between the upper and lower body which helps to redirect the skis into the new turn.

Skidding. The movements used to release the weighted ski (flattening the foot) can also be used to create a skid. Essentially, the difference is that the ski or skis are released but the body does not move in the direction of a new turn. Skidding can be of great value in changing one's turn shape to avoid objects such as rocks or unfavorable patches of snow, or other skiers. Normally, skidding is discussed as a means of speed control. If no room exists to make a turn and a skier must stop, the hockey stop (quickly pivoting the skis sideways) is occasionally the only means of stopping available. At this point, it is a great move.

A certain amount of skidding is present in just about every turn. However, in most skiing situations, the greater the amount of skidding, the less control the skier retains, especially under adverse conditions. Most skiers discover skidding for themselves, and abuse it by overuse, rather than using it appropriately as a tool for special situations.

Lifting the inside ski: Throughout the text we have asked you to minimize the lifting of the new outside ski. This helps minimize gross movements of the upper body and maximize balance. At the advanced level (racing, for example) this lifting can also be observed. At this level it not only releases the old turning ski but provides added room to tip the new turning leg to the inside of the turn.

Soft snow and powder. Increase the intensity of the release to begin your turns as the snow becomes deeper or thicker. It may be helpful to think in terms of "release-release." Once the turn is initiated sufficiently, fresh snow seldom prevents it from continuing. Given the added resistance of these kinds of snow, most of the problems skiers encounter occur when they attempt to add inefficient turning forces and lose their balance. In *extremely* deep or thick snow, it may become necessary to use additional unweighting and specific upper body twisting and to move toward more equalized weighting of the skis. Six inches of fluff requires little or no change.

Hard or icy snow. On hard surfaces skiers may find it helpful to skew their focus toward "engage-engage." The hard snow makes initiating a turn much easier and it therefore becomes the skier's task to quickly and lightly move from ski to ski. A well-tuned ski and special attention to not overpressuring the tip of the ski are both important.

Racing. No matter what the discipline, the fastest skier is normally the one who is able to ride the smoothest, roundest arc with minimal skidding and minimal edging; the one who remains centered and balanced and who allows their equipment to perform at its highest level.

Rebound turning. This type of turning utilizes the release of energy of a ski. The skier allows this energy to build quickly near the end of a turn. The ski bends, forms a platform on the snow, and returns the force back to the skier. From there, the skier normally redirects the force into the next turn. This is an advanced application of skiing skills, and requires the skier to remain centered over the balance spot while quickly allowing pressure to build in the turning ski.

Moguls. Here it is important to have options in terms of possible lines of descent and movements to effectively achieve these lines. The tactics of mogul skiing are very important; however, the bottom line is still the application of fundamentals.

This is obviously a simplistic look at advanced skiing. Quality ski instruction is available throughout the world and becomes more and more valuable to skiers as they progress, and if they hope to continue to grow in proficiency. Look for schools with good reputations and national certification affiliations, and you should do quite well.

A LAST THOUGHT

The difficulty in using this book may lie in the fact that "less is more"—that is, the subtle movements of modern technique produce more effective skiing than the vigorous movements of classic ski technique. Yet it is difficult for many skiers to restrain themselves from doing too much. It is possible to understand intellectually what we are trying to convey and yet abandon it completely when placed in a terrifying ski situation. Therefore, make sure that you internalize the movements you have been learning by practicing them on nonthreatening terrain until they are natural and automatic. Then move gradually to more difficult terrain, expanding your performance envelope in small increments. Don't put yourself in a position where something you have only started to learn has to be called upon to save your hide. You'll probably save it, but with one of Ulle's moves, not with modern technique.

AUTHORS' BIOGRAPHIES

DOUG DECOURSEY has been a full-time ski teacher for nineteen years. He is an examiner for the Professional Ski Instructors of America, Rocky Mountain division. After stints in New York, Vermont, Colorado, southern New Mexico, and New Zealand, the eighties found him writing, teaching, and skiing in Taos Ski Valley, New Mexico. His passion is teaching advanced skiing, particularly in the steeps and moguls.

DARWYN LINDER, Ph.D., is a professor of psychology at Arizona State University, where he works extensively in sport psychology with the university's athletes. He is the author of numerous articles in the *Journal of Personality and Social Psychology*, the *Journal of Experimental Social Psychology*, the *Journal of Sport and Exercise Psychology*, and other scientific journals. He is coauthor of *Psychology Today: An Introduction*, and the forthcoming *A Psychological Analysis of Sport and Exercise Behavior*. He is also a fully certified ski instructor, and served as coordinator of the ski instruction training program conducted jointly through Highlands University and Taos Ski Valley.